W9- βCM - 034

MEN IN BLACKFACE

4670-STAR

MEN IN BLACKFACE

True Stories of the Minstrel Show

Seymour Stark

4670-STAR

Copyright © 2000 by Seymour Stark.

Library of Congress Number: 00-193435
ISBN #:   Hardcover   0-7388-5735-1
                 Softcover   0-7388-5736-X

All rights reserved. No part of this book may be reproduced or transmitted in
any form or by any means, electronic or mechanical, including photocopying,
recording, or by any information storage and retrieval system, without permission
in writing from the copyright owner.

This book was printed in the United States of America.

To order additional copies of this book, contact:
Xlibris Corporation
1-888-7-XLIBRIS
www.Xlibris.com
Orders@Xlibris.com

CONTENTS

Dedicated
to
Nora, Julie,
Darel and Lucas

4670-STAR

THE MINSTREL SHOW WILL NEVER DIE

For most folks the minstrel show disappeared from the American scene with the death of Al Jolson in 1950. Fifty years later Spike Lee resurrected blackface in his film, Bamboozled, as his way to shock into recognition how race plays out now in popular culture.

The reason blackface remains so powerful a symbol of race is its longtime penetration into the consciousness of blacks and whites. The minstrel show, in fact, gave birth to American popular culture in 1843, and continued to influence music, dance, stage and film performance for more than 100 years.

The rise and span of the minstrel show is clearly shown through the lives of the key players, such as P. T. Barnum, Edwin Christy, Dan Bryant, Ned Harrigan, George M. Cohan, Irving Berlin, George Gershwin and Al Jolson.

Blackface portrayal is not solely a racial issue. Ethnic and religious conflict were integral parts of the minstrel show and its progeny (coon songs, musicals and movies). Irish Catholics and Jewish immigrants gained "American whitehood" through the secular stage ritual called the minstrel show.

Five elements identify a ritual (secular as in a courtroom trial or religious as in a funeral).

(1) Repetition of form (format).
(2) Self-consciously "acted" like a part in a play.
(3) "Special" behavior or stylization—the actions or symbols are extraordinary,

(4) Order—an organized event, having a beginning and an end. Order is the dominant mode and is often quite exaggeratedly precise.

(5) By definition ritual has a social meaning. Its very occurrence contains a social message. Ritual symbolizes the social cohesion of the assembled group and simultaneously acts as the vehicle for bringing about social solidarity.

After the Civil War African Americans were recruited into all-colored minstrel shows, but were required to wear the stigma of blackface. In a later period the all-colored minstrel show provided a golden portal to Broadway and the genesis of black dominance in American music and dance.

JIM CROW AND TOM THUMB

Everything known about the evolution of blackface performance from a single clown in a circus act to eight men on stage in a minstrel hall took place in New York City between 1828 and 1847. One man recorded the City's entertainment history in the "colossal, definitive and unique" 15-volume Annals of the New York Stage. George C.D. Odell, Professor of Dramatic Literature at Columbia University, spent 25 years "cataloguing and describing every play...every opera, concert, dance recital, vaudeville and minstrel show" in the metropolitan New York area from 1701 to 1894.[1]

Odell also noted that the first circus in New York City opened on Greenwich Street August 21, 1793. The clown, Mr. McDonald, wore the riding costume of the English equestrian circus. The first uniquely American clown (by the name of George Washington Dixon) appeared in the City in 1828. He was distinguished by the black makeup on his face and the comic love song he wrote and performed by the title of Coal Black Rose.[2]

Over the next three years Dixon had a small vogue as a "negro-singer" at the Chatham Gardens, Park Theatre and Bowery Amphitheatre. Dixon faded from the scene after his performance on May 23, 1831 at the Chatham Gardens, where he sang Coal Black Rose, and "Mr. Weaver, the strong man, bears on his breast 1500 lbs. weight to decide a bet of 500 dollars."

Coal Black Rose, the song that gave Dixon his short-lived fame, became a classic over the next 30 years (published as sheet music and in songsters). The lyrics portray a black lover (Sambo) who visits Rose in the kitchen of her slavemaster. He plucks his banjo while singing (in dialect), "I laff to tink of you as mine, lubly

Rose, I'd gib you a plenty, the Lord above knows, Ob possum fat and hominey and sometime rice, Cow heel an sugar cane an ebery ting nice."

As Sambo confesses his love for Rose, he spys a rival hidden in the corner of the kitchen. The lyrics turn to jealousy and revenge. "What in de corner dar, Rose, dat I py? I know dat nigger Cuffee by de white ob he eye...Let go my arm, Rose, let me at him rush, I swella his two lips like a blacka balla brush." Sambo then vents his anger against Rose. "I wish I may be burnt if I don't hate Rose, Oh, Rose, you blacka snake Rose."[3]

The message of Coal Black Rose for white audiences was that black women were promiscuous and black men were jealous fools. Slavery in the South made romantic love and life-long marriage impossible for blacks. In the North, the blackface performers justified the slavery system by humorous stories about the "natural instincts" of black women. By making Rose Coal Black, white men were supposedly repelled (even though the system made her easily available).

A year after Dixon bowed out of New York City, Thomas D. Rice arrived at the Bowery Theatre on November 12, 1832 as the "sensation of the season." Rice "has drawn crowded houses in Baltimore, Philadelphia, etc.," with his celebrated song Jim Crow. Rice's Jim Crow was the name of a song and the name of a dance (which he performed as he sang).[4]

Jim Crow also had a unique costume: a ragged jacket, mismatched patches on his breeches and a floppy hat. And, of course, his face was covered in black makeup. Rice had established for the first time a total stage character in blackface who was the prototype for the endmen of the minstrel show. His contribution was duly recognized by future minstrels who called him "Daddy Rice."[5]

Jim Crow was meant to be no more than a diversion between acts of a play, but "the famous negro" eclipsed all else as the audience rushed to the stage to join Tom Rice (like a contemporary rock performer). A lithograph, dated 1833, shows Rice surrounded by a mob on stage while the rest of the audience crowds the footlights.

The audience's response to Rice was "unprecedented in the records of theatrical attraction." Identified as "Mr. T.D. Rice of Kentucky," he was actually a native New Yorker who grew up in a City district populated by Irish immigrants.[6]

Rice began his stage career at the Park Theatre, moving scenery and playing small parts. He left New York City for the life of an itinerant player in the new frontiers of Kentucky. At the Southern Theatre in Louisville, he combined acting with stage carpentry and lamp lighting. Rice switched to the Louisville Theatre for a role as a cornfield Negro in a drama. While playing his small part, he had an idea for a blackface song and dance act.[7]

The unrivaled success of Tom Rice led to a slew of articles tracing the genesis of Jim Crow. Seven years after Rice's death in 1860 (start of the Civil War), the Atlantic Monthly traced his brilliant career. The article described in mythic terms the reincarnation of Thomas D. Rice into an "authentic" Negro (at least by song and dance if not by true skin color).[8]

The miraculous event began in Cincinnati when Rice heard "a voice ringing clear and full above the noises of the street, and giving utterance, in an unmistakable dialect, to the refrain of a song to this effect: 'Turn about an' wheel about an'do jis so, An ebery time I turn about I jump Jim Crow.'"

Rice waited until he moved on to Pittsburgh before turning the brief song of an unseen Negro into a performance. Quite by chance as Rice walked by a Pittsburgh hotel on his way to the theater, he encountered Cuff, a Negro attendant. "Slight persuasion induced" Cuff to go with Rice to the theater "where he was led through the private entrance, and quietly ensconced behind the scenes." Rice then "having shaded his own countenance to the 'contraband' hue, ordered Cuff to disrobe, and proceeded to invest himself in the castoff apparel."

On stage Rice sang "O, Jim Crow's come to town, as you all must know, An' he wheel about, he turn about, he do jis so, An' ebery time he wheel about he jump Jim Crow." According to the Atlantic Monthly, "The effect was electric. Such a thunder of applause as followed was never heard before within the shell of that old theatre."

Cuff meanwhile hidden behind the scenes grew impatient waiting for the return of his clothes. After calling to Rice many times, "Cuff in ludicrous undress...rushed upon the stage...called out excitedly: 'Massa Rice gi' me nigga's coat, gi' me nigga's hat, gi' me nigga's t'ings.' . . . the incident was the touch...of such convulsive merriment that it was impossible to proceed in the performance."

Rice's ascendancy as the icon of blackface minstrelsy continued 30 years after his death when The New York Times in 1881 revised the details of the birth of Jim Crow. In the Times account Rice studied the movements of an old and decrepit slave employed in a livery-stable at the back of a theater in Louisville.[9]

The "negro slave was very much deformed—the right shoulder was drawn up high, and the left leg was stiff and crooked at the knee, which gave him a painful but at the same time ludicrous limp. He was in the habit of crooning a queer old tune, to which he had applied words of his own. At the end of each verse he gave a peculiar step, 'rocking de heel;' and these were the words of his refrain: 'Wheel about, turn about, Do jes so, An' ebery time I wheel about, I jump Jim Crow.'"

In the two different accounts of how Tom Rice converted black clothes, song and dance into the persona of Jim Crow, the undercurrent of degradation and pain is "at the same time ludicrous." For the New Yorkers of the 1830s the appalling conditions of slavery were transformed into a parody.

Jim Crow Rice was a hit as never seen before on the New York stage. During the winter and spring of 1833, Rice continued performing Jim Crow and wrote two Ethiopian farce operas, Long Island Juba; or, Love By The Bushel and Oh, Hush! or, The Virginny Cupids. In the hot months of summer New York theaters closed, but in 1833 with Rice's success the Bowery stayed opened "in a flood-tide of prosperity." Rice's "popularity knew no bounds," as he played in whiteface in the role of Hector for Life in Philadelphia, jumped Jim Crow between plays and starred in the Ethiopian opera farce, Oh Hush! or, The Virginny Cupids. The Ethiopian opera had characters by the name of Rose, Cuff and Sambo Johnson, and a chorus which accompanied the stage action with blackface circus songs.[10]

The power of Rice's Jim Crow character transcended the American theater. In 1836 he traveled to London, England, playing Jim Crow every night to audiences at both the Adelphi and Surrey Theatres, "drawing crowds from one to the other to see his act again." Within a month English imitators appeared in theaters. Rice created a character that became a permanent part of the English pantomine. One example was Cowardly, Cowardly, Custard; or, Harlequin Jim Crow And The Magic Mustard Pot, in which Jim Crow turns into a clown.[11]

A review in the London Times in 1836 revealed the strength of the Rice character even when played by another: "Much amusement was excited by Mr. Bedford's appearance (with a song) in the character of Jim Crow; and so excellently did Mr. Bedford personate the 'Yankee Niggar,' that it would be difficult to say which is the funnier presentation of the two—that of Mr. Rice the original or that of Mr. Bedford."

Back in the United States after his rave reviews in England, Rice created new Ethiopian farces with clones of the original Jim Crow. His characters included Ginger Blue in The Virginny Mummy (or the Sarcophagus) and Pompey in Ten Miles from London. Rice starred in a production of Uncle Tom's Cabin at the National Theatre in January, 1854. The play was so popular that two theaters had Uncle Tom's Cabin productions in 1854.

The Spirit of The Times (a newspaper of that time), observed: "Whatever may be the prejudices, political or otherwise, for or against the 'colored bredren' of this country, the feelings provoked by the representation of 'Uncle Tom's Cabin' do us credit . . . 'Uncle Tom's Cabin' holds out yet at the Bowery and National theatres...the performance of this drama has made converts to the abolition doctrine many persons, we have no doubt, who have never examined the subject, and know nothing of its merits."[12]

Among the minstrel men of his day, Rice was acknowledged as the father of the minstrel show. Twenty-four years after he created the "Negro" character of Jim Crow, Rice starred in a rare engagement with Wood's Minstrels in August, 1858. Two years later he died in New York. At the end of his career he was noted for his "eccentricity of dress; the buttons on his coat and vest were five and ten dollar gold pieces, which he would give indiscriminately as souvenirs."[13]

George Washington Dixon and Tom Rice provided the core symbol of blackface for the minstrel show. They also provided the basic concept that parody ruled blackface performance. Parody— in the clown usage to mimic, to mock, to ridicule—guided the minstrel show, giving a smiling face to white racism. Jim Crow (aka "colored") was another Rice legacy.

Eleven years after Rice "jumped" Jim Crow in New York City, Dan Emmett and three blackface companions from the circus created the first minstrel troupe. Billy Whitlock, Dick Pelham, Frank Brower and Emmett were the four who first performed in a minstrel show at the Bowery Amphitheatre in New York City on February 6, 1843. The overwrought words for their public announcement could give them the added honor for the discovery of hype. The four minstrel men invented the style for all subsequent minstrel advertising: "The first night of the novel, grotesque, original and surpassingly melodious Ethiopian Band entitled THE VIRGINIA MINSTRELS."[14]

Since this was the first of its kind, the four minstrels described their offering: "Being an exclusively minstrel entertainment combining the banjo, violin, bone castanets and the tambourine, and exempt from the vulgarities and other objectable features which have hitherto characterized negro extravaganzas."

The Virginia Minstrels acknowledged previous "negro extravaganzas" which raises the question, what was first by the Virginia Minstrels? Credit for the "first" goes to the Virginia Minstrels for the use of the word "minstrels" and an ensemble of four white men in blackface for a full evening of fun. Previously, blackface performance was two men (banjoist with dancer or singer) in the circus or between acts of a play.

George C.D. Odell saw an accumulation of critical mass immediately prior to the birth of negro minstrelsy. "From the last nights of that regime at the Amphitheatre emerged the first band of negro minstrels, inaugurating an art that was to endure for many decades...From my record of the season 1842-43, the reader may see how numerous were appearances, in that term, of blackface comedians. 'Negro' specialists were at the Chatham Theatre, in October 1842, and again in January 1843."

The Franklin, during the autumn and early winter had listed among its attractions "Dan Emmett, Frank Brower, Frank Diamond, and Pierce, the 'heelologist.' And now, on January 14th, the Amphitheatre of the Republic advertised Billy Whitlock and Dan Gardner, in their original Serenade, as well as Madigan in Jim Crow, Esq. on Horseback, with R. W. Pelham as negro clown. G.W. Dixon, 'the Pedestrian and Melodist,' was another entertainer...And within a week thereafter negro minstrelsy, as afterward understood, was born into a jubilant world."

Odell documented the quick succession of blackface clowns (on horseback and on foot) who entertained New Yorkers in the cold January of 1843 before the minstrel show emerged. During the first decades of minstrelsy, over 70 blackface clowns drifted from the circus to the minstrel stage. They had performed in the ring of 28 different circus companies; some notable circus names included Yankee Robinson, Amburgh, Spalding and Rogers, Raymond and Waring, Sam Stickney's, O'Brien's, Gardner and Forepaugh's, Sells Brother's and A.P. Ball's American Coliseum Circus.[15]

In the context of America's growing obsession with race prior to the Civil War, the blackface circus clown reinforced the boundary of separation (the color line). A white man in blackface makeup was a proclamation of his genuine race. The makeup was a "spotlight" on the issue of race. Skin color, however, was an outward sign of the differences between white European and black culture.

The anxiety about black character and culture could not be dealt with by a few blackface clowns in a circus performance. The race issue required an entire theater devoted exclusively to blackface performance. The minstrel show from its inception was America's theater of race. Founded in New York City in 1843 the minstrel show invaded a dozen theaters in the City and spread to Philadelphia and Boston.

In fact, Dan Emmett and the Virginia Minstrels were the first to introduce the minstrel show to Boston at Melodeon Hall. Then on the first day of spring in 1843, the four minstrels sailed to England, performing in Liverpool and Manchester, before spending a month in London at the Adelphi Theatre. Such great success was too much for the men. They choose to disband, and Whitlock sailed back to New York to rejoin the circus.[16]

Emmett, Pelham and Brower met up with Joe Sweeney who was traveling with Cook's Circus in England. Sweeney began his career as a blackface circus performer in the United States about five years earlier. The revived Virginia Minstrels with Sweeney replacing Whitlock traveled to Dublin for a Celtic tour that included Cork, Belfast, Glasgow and Edinburgh. Again, at the end of the tour the group disbanded, but the Virginia Minstrels won a place in history.

Emmett, not destined for fame in New York City, formed a new group called the Legitimate Ethiopian Band. Emmett's band played the hinterlands of Massachusetts during the winter months and worked in traveling circuses during the summer. Although he remained a minor performer in the minstrel show, Dan Emmett achieved immortality for a tune he wrote as a walk-around for the Bryant Minstrels.

His tune, Dixie, became the battle cry of the Confederate army during the Civil War, and remains a symbol of race divisiveness. The word, Dixie, meant for Emmett the black South. In an earlier song by the title of Jonny Roach, Emmett described a runaway slave on the underground railway who "wishes he was back agin...Gib me de place called 'Dixie's Land,' wid hoe and shubble in my hand; Whar fiddles ring an' banjos play, I'll dance all night an' work all day."[17]

Dixie became a popular song in the South after its performance in New Orleans (Emmett never visited the South prior to the Civil War). Once the war started, the South adopted Dixie as its anthem. New words were added to the chorus: "Advance the flag of Dixie! Hurrah! Hurrah! For Dixie's land we'll take our stand, and live and die for Dixie!"

Emmett condoned slavery, but deplored the South's goal of a breakaway confederacy. Twenty-seven years before the Civil War, Emmett joined the army as an 18-year-old infantry recruit. He received training as a fifer and drumer, discharged offically as "a musician." The U.S. Army made Emmett a musician but the Confederate cause adopted him as a hero.

When Emmett died in 1903 no headstone marked his grave. Then in 1931 the United Daughters of the Confederacy donated a memorial to Emmett as the composer of Dixie. It stands in front of the County Building in Mount Vernon, Ohio.[18]

Dan Emmett conceived the first four-man minstrel show that performed on stage for a full evening of music and dance. But within three months his troupe fell apart. Phineas Taylor Barnum, not Emmett, deserves the credit for promoting the craze for minstrel shows. Barnum began his career in show business with Barnum's American Museum in New York City, at the corner of Ann Street and Broadway. His display of human freaks—576 pound Susan Barton, many bearded ladies, 25-inches-high Tom Thumb—plus alligator, giraffes and mermaid drew yearly 400,000 of the curious.[19]

On the same day (September 4, 1843) that he presented General Tom Thumb (world's most famous dwarf), Barnum introduced the Ethiopian Serenaders (an early minstrel troupe) to the crowds at his museum. Barnum delighted in aberrations of nature, as well as outright fakes (the mermaid). In Barnum's mind

were the blackface white minstrels unnatural men? Or were they
entertainers with a vital message for the audience about the nature
of blacks?[20]

About ten years before Barnum promoted minstrels, he owned
slaves while on the road in the South. He suspected his personal
valet stole some valuables. The "nigger" got 50 lashes and was sold
at auction. Barnum defended slavery and opposed the the cause of
the abolitionists. He wrote: "If the blacks were...set free and there
was no army to protect the whites, the blacks would murder them
and take possession of their property."[21]

Two days after General Tom Thumb and the Ethiopian
Serenaders appeared at Barnum's Museum, the competing Peale's
New York Museum presented the Kentucky Minstrels (who shared
the limelight with Madame Adolph, the fortune-teller). Barnum,
so eager to dominate show business in New York City, had bought
out Ruben Peale's museum on condition of strict secrecy. Some
years later, he merged Peale's with his enterprise.

For four years (1843–1846) Barnum controlled more than
half of all minstrel shows in the city by providing two museums as
venues. The Kentucky Minstrels who played at Peale's Museum in
the fall of 1843, made their appearance at Barnum's a year later.
The names of the Kentucky Minstrels appear in a newspaper ad:
Barney Williams, Cool White, T. G. Booth and Billy Whitlock.
Barney Williams (born in Cork, Ireland with the surname of
O'Flaherty) was best remembered for his roles in Irish comic plays.
Cool White (first known in Philadelphia as John Hodges) organized Cool White's Broadway Minstrels in 1870 after many years
in circus rings and minstrel troupes. T. G. Booth left no trace of
his life. Billy Whitlock, a typesetter for the New York Herald by
day and a blackface banjoist at night, was in the first minstrel
show (Emmett, Pelham, Brower). His last public appearance was
with a circus in 1855.[22]

While Barnum monopolized the best venues for freaks and
minstrel shows, new entries for minstrelsy appeared at 15 other
sites in the City (not counting the circuses which always had an

Ethiopian concert). Palmo's Opera House (built specifically for Italian opera) gave its audience a steady diet of blackface opera. Three smaller concert halls (Melodeon, Minerva and the Society Library) provided an assortment of minstrels for a receptive audience. Even at Vauxhall Garden (an outdoor stage) the minstrels performed during the summer. Between Emmett's founding of the minstrel show in 1843 and the first full-time, permanent minstrel hall in 1847, the minstrels took divergent paths.[23]

Could blackface women satisfy an audience? The first female group, Three Sable Sisters (Annette, Angeline and Pauline), made a try at the Apollo Rooms in November 1844. Their featured attraction was A Night with The Darkies. Four days later the Lady Minstrels (no further identification) graced Peale's New York Museum.[24]

Four years after the female experiment at Peale's, the Ethiopian Melodists and Sable Sisters presented "songs, glees and dances and the laughable burlesque, The Colored Fancy Ball." It was fitting that the Sable Sisters staged their Ball at the Hall of Novelty. The last time blackface females tempted a New York City audience (May 10, 1848) only the advertisement was typical minstrelize. Prof. Pesch's Celebrated Band of Female Minstrels; "this is the first band of female minstrels that ever appeared in the United States." The site: Temple of Muses.[25]

P. T. Barnum would try anything once. In May of 1844 his museum offered Juvenile Ethiopian Minstrels, ranging from three to ten years of age. Some 70 years later songwriter Gus Edwards produced the Kids Kabaret, a blackface vehicle for young talent (Eddie Cantor and George Jessel).[26]

Barnum's first venture into minstrel shows with the Ethiopian Serenaders seemed to confirm his instincts for what the public wanted. Between the performance at Barnum's Museum and their next performance in New York City (a year later at the Apollo Saloon), the Serenaders announced they had appeared in Washington "at the President's Private Mansion by Invitation."

By 1845 the Ethiopian Serenaders were booked over and over again at Palmo's Opera House. "The public never tired of (them), the best of the minstrel bands heard up to that time in New York City." In their costumes, the Ethiopian Serenaders were both elegant and refined. No hint of clown disorder in their appearance. In fact, their October 1845 playbill at Palmo's Opera House listed only one instrumental duet (accordian and bones) and no plantation dances. Instead, the evening's three parts overflowed with vocalists (13 individual solos, the full company of five men sang 10 numbers, and a quartet rendered When de Moon is on de Lake).[27]

Early in 1846 the Ethiopian Serenaders sought new audiences in England. Feted by Queen Victoria at a command performance, the Serenaders were the rage in London. Theater critics could not agree. "The most beautiful combination of humour and pathos," wrote one, while another heard "inexplicable and inhuman noises...snores, chokings and whistles." The issue of slavery framed a London newspaper article, March 18, 1846: "Such was the effect produced, not alone upon ourselves, but manifestly upon a vast majority of the listeners...deep commiseration for the unhappy misused beings who, under all the wrongs which they endure, can laugh and sing and dance gaily."[28]

In spite of applause at the White House and the Queen's castle, the Ethiopian Serenaders were not the future of minstrelsy. Edwin Pearce Christy, who first appeared at Palmo's Opera House in New York City February 24, 1846, defined the unique format that lasted 100 years.[29]

In his lifetime (and generations later), Christy was acknowledged as the most important minstrel producer, as well as a talented dancer, singer and burlesque artist. In his first New York performance, he introduced the regulation semi-circle in part one. Christy was the first to place the interlocutor in the center, and place Mr. Bones and Mr. Tambo at each end. He instituted the comic banter between the interlocutor and the endmen. Christy also took credit for the colorful suits of minstrels, the first street parades and for the variety acts of part two (the olio).[30]

Christy learned from Barnum that a building with your name attached would help insure the longevity of his troupe. On March 22, 1847, Christy played to a so-so audience at his new hall on 472 Broadway. By the fall of 1847, Christy played head-to-head with the Ethiopian Serenaders (just returned from "appearing before Queen Victoria, Prince Albert"). The Senenaders stayed at Palmo's Opera House for the month of October.[31]

The Spirit of the Times, in the October 9 issue, stated that a crowded house greeted the returned vocalists, and applauded them "in the most enthusiastic manner...They (Ethiopian Serenaders) are decidedly the most popular artistes in their line in the United States, and by all means the very best singers."

Just a week later (October 16), the Spirit of the Times compared the Christy troupe with the Serenaders. "About the popularity" of the Serenaders, "we draw in. We think the Christy Minstrels are as popular, and that unless the Ethiopians change their performances, will be more popular in a short time...The performances of the Ethiopians as a delineation of Negro eccentricities is a failure. It is entirely too elegant."

The newspaper praised Christy's Minstrels for "the most decidedly original exhibition that we have seen, and accomplish what is the legitimate object of their costumes and colored faces, namely the personation of the witty negro...at the Serenaders opera house, we listen and are pleased, but leave with little desire to return." At Christy's hall, "we listen and laugh, and have a desire to go again and again."[32]

Another week passed, and on October 23, the Spirit of the Times writer described his difficulty in getting into Christy's crowded hall, where he was forced to sit in the third row from the entrance. "Before eight," he wrote, "the middle aisle was full; the entrance crowded, and four or five men perched on the door frame."[33]

Christy's minstrel hall in the next seven years rivalled Barnum's museum as a prime attraction for visitors and the half million New York City residents. Except during the summer months when they traveled (once to England) Christy's minstrel hall always had a line at the entrance. George C. D. Odell wrote about the opening of the season in 1850: "No establishment in New York had a more placid and happy career. There is absolutely no history beyond a record of unfailing popularity and prosperity. Christy's was Christy's; the manager announced the continuance of performances and the public flocked to enjoy. The advertisements specify nothing; it was like a shop so trustworthy that no window display was necessary. Christy's was open for business; the public knew where the best goods were to be bought."[34]

Christy's conception of a minstrel show became the gold standard for future generations of blackface performers. The Ethiopian Serenaders gave their audience blackface vocal music. Christy gave his audiences blackface comedy.

Mr. Tambo and Mr. Bones (as conceived by Christy) were an American varition of the circus clown, who in turn originated with the commedia dell'arte in Italy about 1514 A.D. The commedia produced a number of "zanni" (servant/trickster) who evolved into whiteface circus clowns in France and England. Early in the history of the commedia dell'arte, the nature of zanni character was analyzed. Of two zanni on stage, one must be clever, witty, keen, who can perplex, cheat, trick, and delude every one. He must be cynically sharp, so that his witticisms have in them a spice of risqueness and do not sound merely stupid. The other zanni must be foolish, clumsy, dull, so that he cannot tell his right hand from his left.

The modern version of zanni are Charlie Chaplin, Chico and Harpo Marx (less so Groucho), Stan Laurel and Oliver Hardy. The zanni in France (Harlequin and Pierrot) relied on pantomine and a distinctive costume which gave them instant identification. So too with Chaplin who, in his ill-fitting jacket and baggy pants, added a cane to his wardrobe. Chico wears an immigrant's peculiar jacket and fool's hat. Harpo has his articulate handhorn and long coat with deep inner pockets for gadgets and bananas. Christy's Tambo and Bones should be thought of as early incarnations (in blackface) of Chaplin, the Marx Brother, Laurel and Hardy. (See illustration of the Christy minstrels in performance during 1847).

Besides the immense influence of the commedia's zanni on blackface comedy, there were remarkable similarities between the commedia dell'arte and the minstrel show. No script was used by either. Both were theaters of improvision based on recognizable "types," such as pantolone, the old man in the commedia and zip coon, the blackface dandy.

Mr. Tambo was named for the tambourine, and Flautino in the commedia named for the flute. Elaborate folk dances in the commedia were matched by the minstrel show's ecstatic plantation breakdowns. Just as the banjo became the musical icon of the minstrel show, the mandolin represented the commedia dell'arte. Harlequin wore a black leather mask. His mask was symbolic of his origin as a god of death and his association with the devil. Zanni is a variant on the devil's name (Giovanni) in Italian. Blackface in the minstrel show, however, dealt with the unique American concerns about race.[35]

Why ask a clown to explore the differences between white and black? By their nature, clowns live on the boundary between order and chaos. The traditional European clowns worked in pairs, the whiteface who was refined and "civilized" and the auguste (red nose and baggy pants) who was disruptive and rude. Within the group of minstrels on stage, Mr. Tambo and Mr. Bones were witty but disruptive. They were held in check by the interlocutor. In some early engravings of the minstrel semi-circle the endmen actually wore clown costumes.[36]

The blackface minstrels in the center usually appear in formal attire which matches their refined decorum (knees an inch apart when seated). Depending on their function in the minstrel show, the blackface performers could play the "civilized" role or the rude auguste. One question minstrels posed by these opposite roles was what is the influence of black culture...disciplined (orderly) or chaotic?

There is no precise answer to what the clown does or what his performance means. Centuries before clowns appeared in Europe, the fool in his show often transgressed boundaries between classes or castes...a boundary that separates social order from disorder. His intent was "within the fixed bounds of what is permitted, an experience of what is not permitted." Fools added disorder to order and made an integral whole.[37]

Primitivism (comparing the white European with black African) and a license for sensual movements on stage permitted minstrels to break the puritan taboo against sexuality. Not until 1996 (151 years after its founding in Texas) did Baptist Baylor University permit dancing on campus. Were the minstrels a fool's conduit for integration of black culture into American life? By intent or not, the minstrels were the first to make (counterfeit) black music and dance the essence of popular culture.[38]

IRISHNESS OF IT ALL

Christy's minstrels thrived at the same time that emigration from Ireland transformed New York City. Irish fleeing the famine found refuge in the City, but often the new immigrants shared rooms in a tenement dwelling (two rooms converted into one room each for two families). All the ills of contemporary urban life—crime, alcoholism, proverty, dismal housing, unemployment—were first encountered by Irish immigrants. As Roman Catholics, the Irish were seen as outcasts (espousing anti-democratic popery). Scorned by the Protestant majority, the Irish found solace in the minstrel show. They may be Catholic, but the Irish are certainly white.

Did Christy warm to the Irish of New York City because he had an Irish heritage? Born in Philadelphia (1815), Christy possibly changed the spelling of his surname. What was an Irish family name in Waterford, spelt "Cheasty," may have changed in Philadelphia to Christy. The first record of Christy's exploits place him in Buffalo where he performed as a blackface banjo player. After recruiting three performers for a minstrel troupe, Christy came to New York City. His first public notice (after adding three more men) made the City aware of his arrival: "Christy's far famed and original band of Ethiopian Minstrels...introducing a variety of entirely new songs, choruses and burlesques. Admission 25¢."[1]

The first time Christy performed in New York City (Palmo's Opera House, May 1846) his troupe included "R. M. Hooley."

Years later Richard M. Hooley was the most successful impresario of blackface entertainment. He built minstrel theaters in Brooklyn and Chicago. He managed minstrel theaters in Manhattan, as well as traveling minstrel shows. Hooley, a native of Ballina, Ireland, came to New York City in 1844 and joined up with Christy's in Buffalo. He stayed with Christy for two years. There is no evidence to verify an Irish boys network, nor any to the contrary.[2]

When Christy had his own minstrel hall on Broadway, Hooley was gone. Another Irishman, J. W. Raynor, began a permanent engagement (1847 to 1854) with Christy's blackface comics. Arriving in New York City from Ireland (1833), Raynor several years later made his debut as a vocalist. Next he helped create Campbell's Minstrels. In view of the newspaper critics adoration of Christy during October 1847, a new member of the December troupe (Raynor) must indeed display extraordinary talent (and perhaps a bond with Christy's heritage).

In his second season with the Christy troupe, Raynor had two solos. In part 1 he sang Mary Blane, and in part 2 he presented Sugar Cane Green (probably a song). This early playbill (July 21, 1848) shows the importance of Edwin P. Christy as a performer. It also verifies the great role of Christy's stepsom, George Christy, who adopted his stepfather's surname. When George Christy quit the troupe in 1854 in a dispute with his stepfather, Christy's minstrels loss their standing as the number one minstrel troupe.[3]

Part 1

Overture	the Full Band.
Where is the Spot that We Were Born on, glee by the Company.	
Stop That Knocking, an operatic burlesque	E.P. Christy.
Louisana Belle (a song)	George Christy.
Mary Blane (a song)	J. W. Raynor.
Old Uncle Ned (a song)	George Christy.
Duet for bones and violin	G. Christy and C. Abbott.
We'll Have a Little Dance To-Night	E.P. Christy.
The Phantom Chorus from La Sonnambula	the Company.
Quickstep	the Band.
Original Burlesque Lecture on Phrenology	
	E.P. and George N. Christy.

Part 11

Banjo solo	Earl Pierce.
Banjo duet	E. Pierce and G. Christy.
The Railroad Traveller	Raynor, Pierce and G. Christy.
The Locomotive Overture	the Band.
Way Down South in Alabama (a song)	E.P. Christy.
Jim Crow Polka	George Christy.
Sugar Cane Green	J.W. Raynor.
The Gallery Fire	E.P. Christy.
The Gal with the Blue Dress on (a song)	George Christy.
Way Down in Old Virginia, introducing the Holiday and Festival Dance	George Christy and Earl Pierce.

Part III

Violin solo	C. Abbott.
Accordian solo	H. Donnelly.
Lucy Long	George Christy.
Orginal burlesque polka	G. Christy and Pierce.

Christy's rise to the top, leaving other minstrel shows with his leftover audiences, coincided with the waves of emigrants from Ireland who settled in New York City. Hooley and Raynor left Ireland before the Great Potato Famine (1845-1849). Earlier crop failures and the oppressive reign of British Protestants made America a land of hope for Irish immigrants. Documents in Ireland record five potato famines between 1817 and 1848. Ten years before the Great Famine of 1848, poor potato harvests led to starvation in many areas of Ireland.

Ireland is an island of remarkable statistics. Every second person born in Ireland between 1750 and 1900 had permanently settled in a foreign country. Ireland had the fastest growing population of any European nation, with four and half million in 1790 and over eight million in 1845.

The humble potato allowed the Irish population to nearly double in just 50 years and the blighted potato reduced the population by half. For the poor Irish farmer with no land except for a garden plot, the potato was better than the Biblical manna falling from the heavens.

Potatoes grew easily, even in bad soil, and a single acre could feed a large family. The average family filled up on potatoes every day, plainly boiled with a pinch of salt for taste. The potato feast came to an end in 1845 when a fungus destroyed the potato crop. In the next year the crop was again destroyed by the fungus, and again in the next three years. The Great Potato Famine caused over one million to die of starvation and forced millions more to flee to England, Australia, Canada and the United States.

The government in England did provide relief in the form of soup kitchens, public works projects and food distribution. But for Irish nationalists the inadequate response of British politicians appeared a quick solution to the "Irish Question" by allowing the Irish to starve.

During the worst year of the famine (1847) a new Poor Law stipulated that no peasant was eligible for relief if he held a quarter-acre of land. Large landowners bought small holdings at famine sale prices. The party in power, the Whigs, considered it immoral for the government to give away food, so it established a public works program for the poor to earn the money to purchase food. But the numbers of people (500,000) overwhelmed the program.

The official in charge of relief, Charles Trevelyan, explained his policies: "The great evil is not the physical evil of famine, but the moral evil of the perverse and turbulent character of the (Irish) people."[4]

There was no hope for survival for great numbers of Irish people. In 1847 when the potato crop failure became a way of life, 105,500 Irish immigrated to the United States. Most settled in Boston, Philadelphia and New York City. In the next several years, between 1848 and 1851, immigration from Ireland averaged

164,390 each year. In a short time, the Irish were the largest for-
eign-born group in New York City.[5]

Although the vast majority of Irish immigrants were farmers
and villagers, they settled in the cities. In New York City, the Irish
created the first American ghetto, combining squalor, extreme over-
crowding, the contagion of tuberculosis, mental breakdown, alcoholism and crime. The Irish who fled during and after the famine
years did not disperse into the vast farmlands of the Midwest as
the Germans who came in greater numbers to America.

The Irish were "the first unwanted aliens...hated as papist
subversives," wrote a scholar. In Ireland as Catholics they experi-
enced intolerance from the landlords and officials who were Protestants. In the United States, other Protestants continued the discrimination against the Irish. Every Irish person knew the story of
"Help Wanted" signs with the slogan, "No Irish Need Apply."

A decade before the Great Potato Famine migration, anti-Catholic riots in Philadelphia killed 13 people and two Catholic churches
were burned. In Charlestown, Massachusetts the Ursuline Con-
vent was destroyed by fire.

The Irish immigrant witnessed "Paddy making." An effigy
dressed in rags, sometimes wearing a string of potatoes around its
neck or a codfish to mock the Friday fast, and with a whiskey
bottle stuck in one pocket, was displayed in public on the eve of
St. Patrick's Day.[6]

The Chicago Evening Post expressed Protestant public opinion when it attacked Irish Catholics: "Scratch a convict or a pauper
and the chances are that you tickle the skin of an Irish Catholic at
the same time—an Irish Catholic made a criminal or a pauper by
the priest and politicians who have deceived him and kept him in
ignorance, in a word, a savage, as he was born."[7]

In commemoration of St. Patrick's Day in New York City,
Harper's Weekly cartoonist Thomas Nast portrayed the Irish march-
ers in frock coats and high hats, but their faces were "The Planet
Of The Apes." Caricature ape faces on human bodies were shown
beating the hapless police with clubs or kicking them in the face

when down. The caption read, "Rum and Blood. Brutal Attack on the Police. The Day We Celebrate. Irish Riot."[8]

An Irish-born New York City lawyer John Blake Dillon, pronounced bitterly, "The great majority of the American people are, in heart and soul, anti-Catholic, but more especially anti-Irish. Everything Irish is repugnant to them."[9]

For American Protestants, Irish brutality was the epitome of vile traits that included laziness, immorality, ignorance and superstition. In the 19th century the Catholic Church was the enemy of America's democratic institutions with Irish immigrants as the advance army of papal aggression.

Philadelphia's historian Ellis Paxson Oberholtzer described Irish immigrants in terms of "revolting and vicious habits. Being of the lower order of mankind, they were repellent to those who were further advanced in the social scale."[10]

Some Irish dealt with the hostility from the established Protestant community by filing court petitions to change their Hibernian names. Most closed ranks within their own communities, leading to a subculture and a separatism that estranged the Irish from other groups in the cities.

In Philadelphia they created Irish building and loan associations, often as adjuncts to Catholic churches. Fraternal organizations, fire brigades, neighborhood and workingmen's groups served the Irish-born which made up 21 percent of Philadelphia's population.

Escaping the Protestant oppression in Ireland, the Irish landed in America where Protestants skewered "Catholic popery" and led the campaign for the abolition of slavery. Irish Catholic newspapers in the United States responded against the abolitionists with accusations of "infidels and heretics." The Catholic Telegraph claimed that the Protestant clergy was "at the bottom of the abolition faction."

The Irish News charged Garrison (the leading abolitionist) with advocating free love and treason. The Catholic Mirror of Baltimore pointed with pride to the fact that among 3,500 signers of a petition against the Kansas-Nebraska bill (which restricted slavery in the west), there was not a single priest.

Catholics perceived abolition and anti-Catholicism as part of the same crusade, since the anti-slavery movement was often led by the same Protestants who stirred ill-will against Catholic immigrants.[12]

Slavery was defended by the Catholic Church (the Jesuits in Maryland and the Ursuline nuns in New Orleans owned slaves) which advised slaves to serve their owners in keeping with the teaching of Saint Peter, "Servants, obey your masters." The slave had an obligation under Church teaching to work humbly and obediently according to his lowly state in life.

An Irish Congressman from New York City, Michael Walsh, proclaimed, "The only difference between the Negro slave in the South and the wage slave of the North is that one has a master without asking for him, and the other has to beg for the privilege of being a slave."[13]

While Irish males in the North competed with blacks for jobs at docks and warehouses and in pick-and-shovel gangs, "even the Irish chambermaid looks with jealousy upon the employment of Negro girls in our hotels."[14]

Frederick Douglass wrote about the Irish five years before the Civil War: "every hour sees us elbowed out of some employment to make room for some newly arrived immigrants...white men are becoming house servants, cooks and stewards, common laborers and flunkeys."[15]

From the other side, the Boston Pilot (an Irish newspaper) played to the fears of its readers, "We have already upon us bloody contention between white and black labor...The North is becoming black with refugee Negroes from the South. These wretches crowd our cities, and by overstocking the market of labor, do incalculable injury to white hands."[16]

Newspapers read by Irish Americans had a single theme in their articles, "An African negro and a Caucasian white man can never become equal; not having been made so in the scale of creation."

Another article on the same theme: Negroes under the protection of "gloomy and giddy-brained puritans" behaved themselves with a "swagger of artificial consequence, and an assumption of equality."

An editor wrote, "Why should the sable race of Africa, to whom the inscrutable wisdom of providence has denied the power of intellect, the amenity of the moral affections, and the grace and whiteness of form, presume to enter the lists of human perfection?"

Since blacks lacked the "grace and whiteness of form," Irish Americans embraced white society's obsession with subordination of Negroes. As Catholic outsiders (and for Irish-born as foreigners), the Irish claimed their membership in American society on the basis of their white race.[17]

At the onset of the Civil War, Irish Catholics in the North rallied to the Union cause, forming Irish regiments in Illinois, Massachusetts and New York. A popular jingle expressed the Irish attitude about war and about slavery. "Warm hearts to the cause of our country we bring, To the flag we are pledged—all its foes we abhor-and we ain't for the nigger but we are for the war."

In New York City during 1863, many Irishmen supported neither the war nor Lincoln's Emancipation Proclamation. A new draft law heightened Irish resentment. Under the newly revised rules, a man whose name was picked could pay 300 dollars for a substitute to serve in his place. No Irish laborer had an extra 300 dollars in his pockets.

Due to an offical blunder in assigning draft quotas a greater number of new draftees came from Irish wards in the City. The annoucement of the draft quota came on Saturday, July 11, 1863. On Monday thousands of Irish workers protested by staying away from work. The workmen clustered in angry crowds. The police (a majority of whom were Irish Americans) under Superintendent John Kennedy tried to disperse the crowds, but instead ignited a violent rampage by mobs moving through the city attacking blacks on the streets.

Tuesday's New York Times headline: "The Mob in New York, Conscription Offices Sacked and Burned, Private Dwellings Pillaged and Fired, Colored People Assaulted—An Unoffending Black Man Hung, The Colored Orphan Asylum Ransacked and Burned, A Day of Infamy and Disgrace."[18]

One out of every four New Yorkers in 1863 was born in Ireland. In the same year as the draft riot, the Association for Improving the Condition of the Poor reported that "it remains true as in years past that most of the dwellings of the poor were wretched hotbeds of disease, which are unfit for human habitation."

The tenement dwellings, four to six stories high, provided two rooms for each familiy (one 8 feet by 10 and the other 6 by 10). Sometimes the family would sublet a room. An investigator found a father, mother, and children living together with pigs in a tenement.

When a state committee visited Sweeney's Shambles (the tenants' name for the building), they found four hundred Irish residents in rooms for half that number. In another building on Park Street, close to City Hall, fifty Irish families were counted by authorities. When The New York Times in 1863 described the Fifth Avenue Orphan Asylum for Colored Children as "located in the most pleasant and healthy portion of the City," Irish resentment could be expected.[19]

On the streets of Boston, Philadelphia and New York City, the Irish-born Catholic immigrants faced hostility from the native-born Protestant majority. In the minstrel halls of the cities, Irish audiences found comfort in the comedy that portrayed their real-life economic rivals as lazy, happy-go-lucky darkies.

Irish and Irish Americans not only swelled the audience, but they filled the ranks of the performers on stage. Edward LeRoy Rice published in 1911 the now rare book that identifies over one thousand minstrels. His father, a well-known blackface female impersonator, has three pages in the book. Even the most famous minstrels received a brief papragraph. In spite of Rice's motives to honor his father, his book is a treasure for ethnic origins.

Rice gave the birthplace of each minstrel, and a search of the pages revealed 27 born in Ireland. Many more Irish Americans were identified when Rice's list of names was matched with MacLysaght's The Surnames of Ireland. Those with Irish family names numbered 321.

A common myth told about the minstrels was their Southern origin (that many white performers were born in the South and had firsthand contact with black music and dance). For example, J.W. McAndrews, born in Richmond, Virginia, in 1831, was known as the Watermelon Man. His act, he said, was based on an actual black vendor from whom he purchased clothes and cart.

In truth, only 14 minstrels were born in the South (Alabama, Georgia, Mississippi, South Carolina, Tennessee and Virginia). Nearly twice as many were born in Ireland.[20]

The most influential Irishman among the minstrels was Richard M. Hooley, a native of Ballina, Ireland (County Mayo). Hooley performed with the early Christy troupe in Buffalo and in Christy's first troupe in New York.

Hooley spent his childhood in Ireland, but he grew up in Manchester when the family emigrated to England. Manchester was one of several cities in England with large numbers of Irish.

Hooley's father "was a well-to-do dry goods merchant, who intended his son Richard should become a physician." As a student at Hyde Academy (ostensibly in preparation for a medical career), Hooley had private violin lessons. He "grew quickly to be a phenomenal master of the violin."

Hooley arrived in New York City and apparently by way of an Irish network reached Edwin P. Christy in Buffalo. Hooley, at age 22, was given the "musical leadership of the minstrels." After the debut of Christy's minstrels in New York City, Hooley formed a troupe and returned to England, opening at Her Majesty's Concert Rooms, in Hanover Square, London.

After two years in England, Ireland and Scotland, Hooley returned to America. He next traveled to California to form a partnership with Tom Maguire, an impresario unsurpassed in the cultural life of San Francisco. A native of the Irish slums of New York, Maguire learned the bar trade in the second and third tiers of the Park Theatre (the same theater where Jim Crow Rice served his apprenticeship). His dream was to own a theater and produce classic drama and opera. He followed the gold seekers to the West and opened a saloon and gambling room, and with the profits built a 500-seat theater named Jinny Lind.

At the time Hooley joined Maguire in 1855, the third incarnation of San Francisco's Jinny Lind Theater seated 2,000. Maguire opened another Opera House in 1856, for which he "imported minstrel shows, trapeze artists, novelty programs, and variety acts." Hooley stayed with Maguire until 1858 when he returned to the East.

Ever mindful of the ambitious Maguire across the country, Hooley opened his own theater in Brooklyn in September, 1862. "Hooley's Minstrels, running seven years, and clearing $300,000" had "the most successful record in the annals of negro minstrelsy."

Hooley had the manager's acumen for an expanding business with a new theater and a new audience. He recognized the minstrel show appeal for Irish audiences (and the dominant role of Irish Americans as performers). Brooklyn was an independent city with an Irish population ranked third among American cities.

New York City had by 1870 over 200,000 Irish-born residents. Philadelphia had over 96,000. Brooklyn 74,000. Boston 57,000. Chicago 40,000. And San Francisco 26,000. Each of these American cities had a greater population of Irish-born residents than any city in Ireland, except Dublin.

The Irish communities in America had a network of organizations which traced back to the Friendly Sons of St. Patrick (1784), Irish Emigrant Society (1814), and the first Irish-American newspaper, The Shamrock (1810). No family in Ireland lacked a relative in the United States, and no Irish person in America was unaware of a boarding house in any Irish ward of a city.

With such fabulous success in Brooklyn, Hooley expanded his operations to Chicago in 1869. He constructed Hooley's Opera House on Clark Street. Hooley's foray into Chicago came to a halt in the fall of 1871 when fire destroyed nearly all of the downtown section of the city. His theater was nothing more than scorched rubble.

The great Chicago fire left Hooley with a loss of $100,000. Nonetheless, he sold the land and selected another site on Randolph Street for the new Hooley's Theatre. In less than a year, he opened his theater for the minstrel audiences of Chicago.

By 1878, Hooley decided to resettle permanently in Chicago and sold his Brooklyn theater. "It has been said that he has built, remodeled and managed more theaters than any other manager now living." A.T. Andreas, writing about Hooley in his history of Chicago in 1885, observed that "in a brief biography like this...omitting flattery and personal praise...Mr. Hooley's peculiar ability in managing men and theaters is a natural gift...not in any sense acquired by imitation." Mr. Andreas, partial to an adopted Chicagoian, did not know the influences of Edwin P. Christy and Tom Maguire.[21]

Hooley was the first theatrical manager to recognize a specific Irish audience for the minstrel show. When he selected Brooklyn as the site of his theatre in 1862, the Irish were concentrated in the area known as Irishtown. Brooklyn, as a separate incorporated city, had no bridges to Manhattan at that time.

Manhattan had more Irish, but it also had a dozen theaters with minstrel shows. A theater in Brooklyn, within walking distance of Irishtown, was for Hooley an exclusive franchise.

Irishness was not an advertised element of the minstrel show. Except for Dan Emmett and Richard Hooley with recognizable Irish names, many performers used stage names. Dan O'Brien appeared on the stage as Dan Bryant. Mr. Slattery of Cashel, Ireland performed in New York City as T.M. Hengler. George Delaney and William Flynn were famous as the minstrel team of Primrose and West.[22]

Just as Richard M. Hooley left the Christy Minstrels to start his own group, many other performers engaged in minstrel musical chairs, always seeking a better spot in a new troupe. One such change had tragic results. George Christy, the stepson of Edwin P. Christy and the bright star of the troupe, abandoned the Christy Minstrels in 1853. He formed a partnership with Henry Wood at 444 Broadway, only steps away from Edwin P. Christy's minstrel hall.[23]

The elder Christy hired Jerry Bryant from Henry Wood's troupe, as a repalcement for his stepson. Jerry's younger brother, Dan, also performed in the Henry Wood company. With the loss of his stepson, Edwin P. Christy lost much of the brilliance of his productions. Edwin P. Christy committed suicide several years later at age 47.

The same week Jerry Bryant replaced George Christy at Christy's minstrel hall, brother Dan (Bryant) paired with George Christy in Wood's Minstrel Hall (performing the Cocoanut Dance). Jerry Bryant remained with Edwin P. Christy's troupe about six months before he rejoined Wood's Minstrels and brother Dan.

In a September 1853 program, Jerry Bryant sang Nancy Till and Dan Bryant sang The Gal with the Bloomers on. Dan also had a dance solo: The Grapevine Twist. George N. Christy was the recognized star of Wood's Minstrels, but Dan Bryant was gaining ground.

For the Christmas season of 1853, George Christy sang Jolly Old Crow. Then in Part III, Dan Bryant performed with George Christy in a burlesque opera, The Black Cupids. Soon after the New Year, Dan Bryant's name disappeared from the playbills. George C.D. Odell wrote: "We have missed Dan Bryant…of course no minstrel company was big enough to hold two such giants of minstrelsy as Bryant and (George) Christy."

Nearly a year passes before Dan Bryant showed up in New York City again. He was on the road with the Campbell Minstrels who had an engagement at St. Nicholas Hall (New York City) in July 1855. Dan Bryant stayed in New York City under the banner of Bryant and Mallory's Campbell's Minstrels. Odell anticipated the future: "Dan Bryant, even then boldly advertised as 'the unapproachable Ethiopian comedian, the original essence of Old Virginny,' was heading toward the acclaim which was to make him the idol of the public."[24]

Dan Bryant and brother Jerry would carry on the legacy of Edwin P. Christy who was abandoned by his stepson George. Four years after Dan Bryant and George Christy shared the stage at Wood's Theater, the Bryant Brothers took possession of Edwin P. Christy's minstrel hall at 472 Broadway. For the next 18 years (1857 to 1875), the number one name in minstrelsy was Bryant (known to Irish insiders as O'Brien).

At last on February 23, 1857, the Bryant Minstrels (the brothers Jerry, Dan and Neil) took possession of Edwin P. Christy's famous minstrel hall at 472 Broadway. Odell found a December 28, 1857 playbill for the Bryant Minstrels.

Part First

Grand overture (Elside Norde)	Bryant's Minstrels
Opening chorus (Hark again Thrilling Horn) Company	
Ballad (Gentle Annie)	T.B. Prendergast
Comic (The Aristocratic Darkie)	Jerry Bryant
Ballad (Cottage by the Sea)	W. Percival
Pathetic (Only 19 Years Old)	Dan Bryant
Operatic (Fair Shines the Moon To-night) N.W. Gould	
Refrain (The Darkies' Cheer)	S.E. Clark
Finale (See, Sir, See, Sonnambula)	Percival and Troupe

Part Second
Terpsichorean Divertissement

Ethiopian Fling, a la Rolla	M. Leslie
Congo Coca Dance	Quinn, Jerry and Dan Bryant
Flutina Fantasia	Neil Bryant

Cinquetemps—master and pupil	M. Leslie and Jerry Bryant
Larboard Watch—vocal duet	Percival and Prendergast
Mullhauer Brothers—burlesque violin	Isaacs and Sivori
Tyrolean Warblers	Prendergast, Jerry and Dan Bryant
Essence of Old Virginny—plantation dance	Dan Bryant
Guitar solo—operatic medley	N.W. Gould

Part Third
Plantation Holiday Sports

Plantation banjo song	Dan Bryant
Power of Music—Southern scene	N.W. Clark and Dan Bryant
The Three Hunters	Neil, Jerry and Dan Bryant
The Challenge Dance	Jerry and Dan Bryant
Pastimes on the Levee	W. Quinn

Jerry Bryant's trained elephant, Shelbark,
in his astonishing feats.
The performance to conclude with the laughable
Burlesque Circus and Terrific Horse Combat, introducing
Jerry, Neil and Dan Bryant and their model troupe.[25]

Four years after the opening of the Bryant Minstrels in their own Broadway theater, Jerry Bryant died at age 33. Brother Neil (two years younger than Dan) took Jerry's place in the song and dance acts.

"Bryant's, still the most fixed of the minstrel organization of the city, re-opened on August 5, 1861 for the usual season of dusky mirth and melody," wrote Odell.

In the summer of 1864 Dan Bryant began his personal transformation from New York City's most popular impersonator of the Negro to a quest for his Irish identity. He starred in two theater comedies, The Irish Emigrant and Handy Andy. "Dan Bryant having triumphed in Irish comedy at Wallack's, returned to the

burnt cork, on September 12, 1864, when Bryant's Minstrels began the winter campaign" at 472 Broadway," wrote Odell.

The next year in the summer, Dan Bryant appeared in five
plays, The Irish Emigrant, Born to Good Luck, The Colleen Bawn,
Handy Andy, Bould Boy of Glengail and Shamus O'Brien. In
Shamus O'Brien, Dan Bryant played four different roles: Shamus
O'Brien, Owney Dugan, Denny Doyle and Highen O'Leary.[26]

The 1865-1866 season started late for the Bryant Minstrels as
Dan Bryant was busy with Irish roles. The next year he closed his
minstrel show in the spring in favor of Irish comedy. He took his
Irish plays overseas for an engagement in Dublin. Bryant also performed in Liverpool, a city filled with Irish immigrants. (Irish-
born in Great Britain rose during the famine years from 49,000 in
1841 to 734,000 in 1851).[27]

The Dublin Freeman's Journal (May 30) stated, "Mr. Dan
Bryant, the celebrated Irish comedian, appeared in the Theatre
Royal, Dublin, last evening, for the first time in this country...Mr.
Bryant in delineating that most difficult of characters, an Irishman,
were fully realized last night...Mr. Bryant's 'brogue' (the great
difficulty to all who essay Irish character) is singularly natural...In
the course of the piece he sang, in capital style, 'Finnegan's Wake,'
in which he was encored, and he also treated the house to an Irish
jig, which the audience also insisted on having repeated...Mr.
Bryant...achieved a complete success on this his first appearance
before the Dublin public...A better Irishman has not been seen
on the boards of the Theatre Royal for a long time."[28]

The pilgrimage to "Mother Ireland" was an act of redemption
for his parents, his dead brother, and all the Irish exiles in America.
Back in New York City, Dan Bryant formed an alliance with the
Irish cronies of Boss Tweed's Tammany Hall. In 1868 the Tammany
Democrats opened a new $300,000 headquarters on East 14th
Street near Irving Place. Besides the Grand Hall (seating for 3,500),
the brick and marble building held a library, a club room, committee rooms and a restaurant. A concert room with its own entrance became the home for the Bryant Minstrels.

The Irish political ascendancy in New York City came after a 20-year struggle between Irish Catholics and American-born Protestants. In the spring of 1850 a secret society by the name of The Supreme Order of the Star-Spangled Banner was founded in New York City. Its sole purpose was to plot the political demise of any candidate for political office who held out his hand to Irish Catholics. Eventually, the secret society joined a national political organization (American Party or "Know-Nothings").

During the 1853 elections, the New York Tribune exposed the plot, "this ticket is the work of the managers of a secret organization. It is in fact a disguised form of Native Americanism aiming to control the elections of our city . . . It is essentially anti-foreign, especially anti-Irish and anti-Catholic."[29]

Dan Bryant's alliance with Boss Tweed and his Irish colleagues (John Kelly, Richard O'Gorman, Jimmy O'Brien) was a marketing decision. Tweed's control of the city's politics depended on Irish immigrants transformed "overnight" into naturalized citizens by judges on Tammany's payroll. The brightest of the Irish-born managed to vote a dozen times the same day at different voting sites using assumed names. Many of the Irish were rewarded by jobs. Boss Tweed made Tammany Hall a safe haven for the immigrants, so Bryant's concert hall became a package deal for the Irishmen of New York City: jobs, handouts, citizenship and entertainment by a fellow Irishman who lampooned the lowly African American.

John Kelly, the former sheriff of the city, replaced Boss Tweed in 1868 as head of Tammany Hall. Richard O'Gorman, born in Ireland, had joined an insurrection against the British under the banner of "Young Ireland." The rebellion failed, but O'Gorman escaped to the United States. His reputation as an Irish patriot led to work for Boss Tweed (rallying for the North in the Civil War and for Tammany Hall candidates). In 1865 Tammany backed his election for the City's Attorney post. Jimmy O'Brien, who replaced Kelly as sheriff, managed the Irish voters who visited a dozen polling sites under false names (entered by O'Brien on the registration rolls).[30]

Dan Bryant stayed in the concert rooms of Tammany Hall for two years while he planned the construction of a new theater on West 23rd Street dedicated to the minstrel show. At its opening on November 23, 1870, the four story building could seat over 1,000 in the orchestra and balcony. Bryant's optimistic expectations for the minstrel show in the decade of the 1870's were not shared by New York audiences. By the spring of 1873, Dan Bryant's Opera House was "the only minstrel hall remaining open." Two years later Dan Bryant was dead at age 42.

Bryant, who accumulated a large debt, died broke. In recognition of Bryant's role in sustaining the minstrel show, a massive one-day benefit was held at eleven theaters on April 29, 1875. Also, a public subscription fund (led by The New York Times) raised $22,000 for his widow and children.

The obituary for Dan Bryant in The New York Times (April 11, 1875) mentioned his dual roles as Irish comic in plays and his blackface minstrel dances and skits. Ultimately, "He did not feel 'at home,' however, in white face," observed the Times writer. Born in America, Dan Bryant could not hold on to his Irish heritage (a better Irishman than others when in Ireland) and fulfill his destiny as a white man in America on behalf of the Irish immigrants.[31]

Dan Bryant's influence on the next generation of showmen came at a performance of Bryant's Minstrels at 472 Browadway where 15-year-old Ned Harrigan sat in the audience. Encouraged by his mother to see the minstrel greats of his day, Harrigan defied his father, a ship carpenter (who wanted Ned to do the same).

Born 1845 in New York City's 7th Ward (an Irish enclave along the East River), Harrigan wrote "I learned most of my Negro business and old songs" from my mother. Both his parents were born in New York City, but his grandmother came from Cork, Ireland. His mother, Ellen Harrigan, passed her love of dance and song to her children.

In the evening in the parlor, she led the children in "Southern" songs (she had never ventured below the Mason-Dixon line). The home entertainment ended in a minstrel walk-around, with teenage Ned playing the banjo (lessons from his mother). Harrigan emphasized that his mother "had a capital dialect and could dance and sing 'Jim Crow' as well as I ever saw it done." Many minstrel men claimed an overnight surreptitious visit to a plantation where they learned songs and dances directly from Negroes of the South. Harrigan made clear that black song and dance performed on the stage by whites was a theatrical convention passed from minstrel to minstrel.

Harrigan, indebted to his mother for the minstrel show, found inspiration in his neighborhood for a new brand of comedy (based on ethnic rivalry) which later made him the sensation of New York. The census numbers showed a hand-full of native-born families, contrasted with 812 Irish, 218 Germans, 189 Poles and 186 Italians.

Apprenticed to his father in the shipyard, Harrigan ran away from home after his mother died and his father remarried. He settled in San Francisco, and joined a shipyard crew. Harrigan practiced his blackface song and dance routines for fellow workers who encouraged him to enter an amateur night. The thunderous applause of the shipyard workers convinced a theater manager to sign on the novice performer for San Francisco's Olympic Theater.

Harrigan formed a partnership with Alexander O'Brien and toured the Western states. When the team split up, Harrigan performed as a solo act. At the Winter Garden Theatre in Chicago, Harrigan found his future partner in comedy, Tony Hart. Born in Worcester, Massachusetts, Hart dropped his family name (Cannon). His parents had emigrated from Ireland during the Great Potato Famine of the 1840s.

Four years after the final performance of Dan Bryant in 1875, Harrigan evolved a new theatrical form that mixed Irish and German ethnic comedy with traditional blackface characters from the minstrel show. Growing up in an immigrant neighborhood gave Harrigan his ethnic models for stage characters. The hard-drinking, loudmouthed though lovable Irishman vied with the slow-witted German.

Harrigan and Hart altered the structure of the minstrel show by replacing the first part (Mr. Bones and Mr. Tambo) with New York City ethnic skits. Since the skits ran about 20 minutes, the olio (variety acts) filled out the program. An occasional song tied to the plot and characters replaced the long line of tunes that stood alone on the minstrel program. Harrigan created a deviant offshoot that did not influence other minstrel troupes (and amateurs) who carried on the ritual conceived by Edwin P. Christy and passed to Dan Bryant.

Harrigan and Hart leased the Theatre Comique where they developed their farcical skits, playing off Irish against blacks and Germans against all, as the public clamored for more and more. On January 13, 1879, The Mulligan Guard Ball premiered at the theater. Then over the next two years the Mulligan Guard was at the center of a series of seven plays (all with Mulligan in the title).

In the decade after the Civil War, dozens of "target companies" emerged in New York City, mostly manned by immigrants who were excluded from the regular militia. On Sundays the "target companies" (Mustache Fusileers, Washington Chowder Guard, First Ward Magnetizers) marched with a hired band to the Battery for a boat to Staten Island. The main events of the day were a picnic followed by competitive target shooting (and competitive drinking bouts). Not infrequently, disputes between companies were resolved by fierce riots.[33]

Harrigan's Mulligan Guard was a parody of the immigrant "target companies," with biased sympathy for the boisterous Irishmen. The first performance (Mulligan Guard Ball) pitted the Irish against the blacks for possession of a dance hall. The German proprietor (known for his absent mindedness) had rented the hall to both the Irish Mulligan Guard and the black Skidmore Guard. The Skidmore Guard, led by barber Simpson Primrose and Brother Palestine Puter, is sponsored by the Ancient Order of Full Moons ("de colored secret society pledged to prevent the Irish from riding on the horse carts").

The Mulligan Guard, arriving first at the Harp and Shamrock ballroom, begin their celebration with a song, Babies on Our Block (a litany of Irish names). Then the Skidmore Guard file into the ballroom, carrying muskets. Captain Primrose orders his men to stash their weapons in the hat rack, but keep their razors handy. Primrose warns his men: "Dar's no telling how many Irish will be in hambush dare."

The two camps try at first to share the dance floor, but a melee erupts, women scream, Skidmores draw razors. The German proprietor manages to head off the mayhem by offering a compromise. The Skidmores can move upstairs to the Red Men's Lodge room, with a $10 refund. Captain Simpson says, "as long as we're upstairs—we're above de Irish—and I know dat suits every Full Moon in de company."

As the dancing in the upper quarters gains in tempo, the ceiling sags and plaster falls on the Mulligan Guard. Suddenly the ceiling caves in and bodies fall on the Irish (Harrigan used dummies). This scene represented the epitome of Harrigan's physical comedy and the core of the conflict between blacks and Irish.

Harrigan wrote a march tune for the Skidmores (white actors in blackface makeup): We represent the members of/ De noble colored troops/ Who march about de streets of York/ In French imperial suits/ Black pantaloons and yaller strips/ And helmets trimmed in blue/ De wenches shout when we turn out/ on South Fifth Avenue…Talk about your Mulligan Guard/ Dese nigs dey can't be beat/ We march to time, we cut a shine/ Just watch dese darkies feet/ De left foot first, de right foot follow/De heel down mighty hard/ Ten platoons of dandy coons/ March in the Skidmore Guard.

In the Mulligan skits, Harrigan plays the leader of the Guard. As Dan Mulligan he is an ex-Civil War veteran who owns a corner grocery. He displays the Irish qualities of a good talker and a warmhearted man. A generation before when minstrel star Dan Bryant tried to claim his Irish heritage, he took roles that portrayed the Irish in Ireland, even traveling to Dublin for performances.

Harrigan found his inspiration in the lives of New York City's Irish Americans. The Irish had come out in the open at the Theatre Comique as sympathic characters. When contrasted with the blacks (from the blackface minstrel types), the Irish were an admirable people. Harrigan had rescued the Irish from the charade of blackface where men became white because they appeared black.

Harrigan had turned blackface performance into a vehicle for Irish American comic drama while retaining the boundaries of the minstrel show. His delineation of ethnic characters opened the way for the next generation of Irish Americans who eventually broke completely with the blackface tradition.[34]

George M. Cohan, whose grandparents emigrated from Ireland, professed his debt to Ned Harrigan. Cohan wrote, "Harrigan inspired me when I applauded him from a gallery seat. Harrigan encouraged me when I first met him in after years and told him of my ambitions."

One link between Harrigan and Cohan was the Mulligan Guard plays that introduced songs tied to the characters and plot of the play. Harriagn also was the first to portray the lives of the Irish in America and dramatize New York City's ethnic cauldron. Cohan squeezed the complex world of New York City into a single street, Broadway. Harrigan was still alive in 1905 when Cohan wrote Give My Regards to Broadway. Cohan transformed Harrigan's Irish characters into a new breed of super-patriot Americans (who walk and talk like Cohan himself). While Harrigan's Mulligan Guard did wave an American flag in one hand, the other carried the Irish flag.

George M. Cohan's father, Jerry, was the most enduring influence on Cohan as performer and playwright. Jerry Cohan began his stage career as a blackface song and dance man in minstrel shows. He carried his blackface act into the vaudeville circuit, writing his own songs and skits, and staging his dances. When Jerry married, he convinced his wife (Nellie) to join him in a duo though she never faced an audience. From time to time when the blackface business was slow, Jerry and Nellie performed in Hibernicons, an all-Irish entertainment of music and dance.

The team of Mr. and Mrs. Jerry Cohan grew into a foursome with the birth of Josie (Josephine) in 1876 and George Michael on July 4, 1878. Born on the 4th of July was the theme of his later works. Before he could complete his first year in a Providence, Rhode Island public school, George and Josie joined their parents on a vaudeville tour. From that day George learned all there was to know about show business, and the theater was the center of his universe thereafter.

George earned his keep by selling song-books in theater lobbys, and eventually played the violin in the orchestra. His sister, a talented dancer, worked with the parents on stage. George, eager to be part of the act, tried a trick violin solo which lasted one week. When George was eleven, father Jerry created a full-evening's show that had parts for all the members of the family (calling themselves The Cohan Mirth Makers). Over the next two years the Cohans traveled the country, giving one-night stands in some 600 theaters.

With new skits, the family again went on the road (the Southern tour, the Chicago tour, the Eastern seaboard tour) under the billing of The Four Cohans. Never the starring act, they usually opened the show when the audience had not settled in. Their engaement at the Hyde and Behman's Theater in Brooklyn was a startling exception. Though assigned as the opening act (17 minutes on stage), the Cohans ran 26 minutes because of the audience's demand for encores. With the audience applauding and calling out "Speech, Speech," George stepped forward and bowed low. He gave the curtain speech that became his trademark: "Ladies and gentlemen, my mother thanks you, my father thanks you, my sister thanks you, and I thank you."

The success of the Four Cohans in Brooklyn led to a contract with B.F. Keith who controlled bookings to all of the nation's first-class vaudeville houses. The Cohans were rewarded with the top salary for a four-act. The family's success was matched by George in his creative energy, composing songs. May Irwin, a star of vaudeville, made Cohan's Hot Tamale Alley the featured song of her act. Though only 15, Cohan had already written three hit songs: Venus, My Shining Love; Hot Tamale Alley; and You're the Warmest Baby in the Bunch. The last two were "coon songs," a popular genre inspired by the minstrel show.

In the 1942 film biography, Yankee Doodle Dandy (based on Cohan's talks with the script writers), the Four Cohans perform a blackface song and dance routine. George M. Cohan's fascination with the blackface minstrel show reappeared when he was 31 years old. Having a string of successful plays (with three of his most famous songs), Cohan produced in 1909 the largest minstrel show of that era. He did not perform with the minstrels, but worked with "Honey Boy" Evans on the blackface production.

Jerry Cohan, a product of the minstrel show, proclaimed his Irish identity when he danced a jig in the occassional Hibernicon. His son George moved away from both the minstrel show and Irishness in his stage productions. As script writer, composer, star of the play (frequently) and director, the younger Cohan sought a 110 percent American identity. In the 1904 Little Johnny Jones, Cohan (in the starring role) creates the persona of an American in London who confronts the life-styles of the British. The song Yankee Doodle Boy was a result of that confrontation. On his return voyage to America, Johnny Jones sees New York Harbor which inspires Give My Regards to Broadway.

Two years later Cohan stared in his play, George Washington, Jr., as a young man so obsessed with his "American identity" that he changes his name. The memorable song of that play was It's a Grand Old Flag. The final transformation of the Irish (in the Cohan clan) into a new identity as "American" took 61 years from the start of the mass migration from the Great Potato Famine. Most Irish Americans caught up with Cohan during the Second World War when the four Sullivan Brothers (all killed in the Pacific) epitomized patriotic dedication.

In 1936 the United States Congress awarded George M. Cohan a gold Medal of Honor for meritorius service in World War I. The service specified by Congress was composing Over There and It's a Grand Old Flag. In 1917 Cohan's Over There was the most played song in America. Cohan, the only composer to be honored by Congress, remains the quintessential Broadway song and dance man shorn of blackface, leaving his Irish heritage in the back shadows of the stage.

The blackface minstrel show helped the Irish to assimilate (as white men) in a nation obsessed with racial boundaries. Simply being white was not enough for Dan Bryant (O'Brien) and Ned Harrigan. They needed an Irish identity in America. Cohan never entirely abandoned his Irish heritage. In 1908 he wrote the play, Fifty Miles from Boston, with a song dedicated to Ned Harrigan by spelling his name: H-A double R-I-G-A-N. From time to time an Irish name became the theme of a play. In 1911 he wrote Hogan's Millions, and Honest John O'Brien appeared on Broadway in 1916. Finally in 1923 he wrote The Rise of Rosie O'Reilly.[35]

The Irishmen in the blackface minstrel show claimed an insightful knowledge of black culture. In truth, African Americans created a humorous folklore based on the "numskull doings of immigrant Irish" which augmented the Brer Rabbit tales. In both the North and South jokes about the Irish flourished among black workers. Writer Lafcadio Hern in 1876 described black stevedores on the Cincinnati levee who "mimic the Irish accent to a degree of perfection which an American, Englishman or German could not hope to acquire."

Later in 1923 a folklore expert collected jokes about the Irish from blacks in Philadelphia, and compared those jokes with others about the Irish among blacks in Alabama, Mississippi and Louisiana. Irishman stories were a staple of black humor in Philadelphia (home to a large Irish community) and in the deep South (where a small contingent worked in a few seaport cities). The folklore expert wrote: "It is curious to hear a native-born southern Negro telling a story about Pat and Mike with all the spirit and even the inflection of voice that one might expect of an Irishman."

One example of black humor at the expense of the Irish concerns two Irishmen who buy their first watermelon and give the heart to nearby blacks, but keep the rind for themselves. "Guts is good enough for Naygurs." Historian Lawrence W. Levine explained Irish jokes as "a means of taking revenge upon these newcomers who had learned to hate Negroes so quickly and efficiently. Perhaps more importantly, they allowed Negroes to openly ridicule and express contempt for white people. The Irish characters of black jokelore became surrogates for all the other whites against whom it could be dangerous to speak openly."[36]

M R T. RICE

as

THE ORIGINAL JIM CROW

Thomas D. Rice created the first
stage caricature of the happy slave
who inspired performers in the
minstrel show (Circa 1832).

The Ethiopian Serenaders, the renowned minstrel troupe in 1845 and 1846, performed in the White House and for Queen Victoria in England.

An engraving depicts the comic
blackface antics of Christy's troupe
at their Broadway theater in 1847.

Poster for Dan Bryant's famous blackface Essence of Old Virginny plantation dance. Note the hands drawn as the claws of a beast.

A soulful portrait of Dan Bryant as
the Irish character Shamus O'Brien.

Irving Berlin's 1909 hit, Do Your
Duty Doctor, maintained the racist
message of "coon songs."

In 1896 the Bully Song was one of a series of "coon songs" that depicted black men as brutes.

Al Jolson in the 1934 Wonder Bar
film created Hollywood's most
spectacular blackface production.

IRVING BERLIN TITILLATES

Irving Berlin at age 22 (hailed as the "King of Ragtime") attended his first Friar's Club banquet at the Hotel Astor. The most notable members at the banquet included George M. Cohan, his father Jerry and the minstrel performer Lew Dockstader. Cohan introduced the new member, describing him as "a Jew boy that had named himself after an English actor (Henry Irving) and a German city." Cohan's words seem jarring now, but in a New York City ruled by ethnic identity such words expressed affection. Cohan praised Berlin for writing "a song with a lyric, a lyric that rhymes, good music. He is a wonderful little fellow, wonderful in lots of ways."[1]

Nothing in Irving Berlin's life experience (an immigrant who left school at age 14) prepared him for his speech to the Friars. When he walked to the podium, a pianist hidden behind the curtain played a syncopated melody as Berlin sang satirical lyrics for the occasion. Some months later when the Friar's sponsored their annual Frolic in the form of an old-time minstrel show at the New Amsterdam Theatre, Berlin stopped the show with encores for his new "coon song," Ephraham Played Upon the Piano (a blackface chorus sang along).[2]

Israel Baline came to the United States with one fearful image of Jewish life in Russia. He could remember his family fleeing in the night as fire engulfed their home. By morning the Baline home and other Jewish homes in Mohilev were mounds of ashes. Secret groups financed by a vehement anti-Semitic government organized pogroms against Jews throughout Russia, often killing men and raping women. The Balines, thankful for their lives, left Russia for an uncertain future in the United States.

Moses Baline, the father, was the cantor in Mohilev's orthodox synagogue, the same post held by his father and grandfather. New York City, with surplus cantors from Russia, had no synagogue for 47-year-old Moses Baline. He found part-time work as a kosher poultry inspector and learned the trade of house painting. Moses could not earn enough to support his family. Mother Lena worked as a midwife. The three girls (Rebecca, Sarah and Chasse) rolled cigars in their three-room tenement. The elder son, Benjamin, worked in a clothing sweatshop. Izzy peddled newspapers.

After six years of disappointment in New York City, Moses Baline died of "chronic bronchitis terminating in exhausion." Izzy had celebrated his bar mitzvah two months earlier. The loss of the father's wages from part-time work cancelled any hope that the Baline family would leave the tenement.

Izzy, who could legally quit school at 14, decided he had to live on his own away from his mother. He didn't tell her his plans, but began a new life on the streets. He justified abandoning his mother by the excuse, one less mouth to feed. Years later he revealed his feelings about life with the family. It was not poverty that caused the 14-year old to flee his family. He was an outsider in the United States because, "we spoke only Yiddish and were conspicuous for our 'jew' clothes."[3]

Walking on the Bowery from McKeons saloon to "The Morgue" and on to Donovan's, Izzy sang the popular ditties for the patrons who threw him a penny or two. If at the end of a day he had 15 cents, he stayed in a flop house (bare mattress, sheets 25 cents more). In time he would know the saloons where more pennies landed at his feet. Off Bowery, near the waterfront, on a Saturday night, Izzy earned 50 cents at MacAlear's saloon.

Bowery saloons provided more than beer and gin. Back rooms offered gambling, prostitutes and opium smoking. For two years Izzy had an education in degradation on the Bowery. He hoped that music could lift him out of the squalor. Izzy divided the Bowery between "The bums and riffraff (who) stayed and died off" and others "like myself only waiting to get the hell out of here."

Through the influence of a local politician (who spent much time in the saloons), Izzy found his first full-time job at the Pelham Cafe on Pell Street. Pelham's Cafe was known to all as "Nigger Mike's." Mike Salter, a Russian Jew with a swarthy complexion, made the cafe the headquarters for small-time political graft. Situated in the center of Chinatown, Nigger Mike's catered to tourists in search of adventure among criminals and opium dens. The cafe (a dance floor and bar) had a brothel upstairs and an "opium fiend" known as Chinatown Gertie. For 50 cents extra, the tourists visited Gertie's shadowy room where in her kimono she inhaled from the opium pipe.

Employed as a singing waiter, Izzy earned $7 a week (plus tips), but his work duties started at eight in the evening and ended six in the morning. Within a few months, the new singing waiter was as popular among the tourists as Chinatown Gertie. After midnight on a Saturday in November of 1905, a group of foreign tourists headed by Prince Louis Battenberg (related to England's King Edward) visited Nigger Mike's. The Prince's entourage included two detectives and 18 newspaper reporters. In front of the royalty and the reporters, Nigger Mike introduced "two waiters, called Izzy and Bullhead," as "the best singers in Chinatown." After their song, the pair served beer to the Prince and his party. The royal visit to Chinatown made front-page news, and New Yorkers learned that "Izzy" was a featured singing waiter.[4]

The long hours led Izzy to doze during lulls at the Pelham Cafe. One nap cost his job. While asleep, head pillowed in his arms on the bar, he failed to catch the culprit who snatched the cash from the till. Nigger Mike, in an uncommon rage, booted Izzy out the door.

His name and standing as a singing waiter in the newspapers made Izzy's job search easy. Jimmy Kelly, an ex-boxer and bouncer at the Pelham, opened an uptown restaurant on 14th Street and Union Square. Izzy continued his performances in the new venue at Kelly's. He also decided that he wanted to write his own songs, but he could not read or write music. At first he worked with the pianist at Kelly's, humming a melody while the pianist transcribed it. He never learned how to transcribe music during the next 50 years of productive life, relying on others to write his melodies.

Still working at Kelly's to pay the rent for an apartment he shared with another young songwriter, Berlin teamed up with a number of composers. They wrote the music and he wrote the lyrics. A new music publishing company, Waterson & Snyder, bought his lyrics for an ethnic Italian song. He hummed the music for the company's pianist to transcribe. He then wrote another ethnic song, Sadie Salome, Go Home (Sadie Cohen is a striptease dancer who uses seven veils). Sadie sold 3,000 copies and gave Berlin a new job as staff lyricist. His salary jumped from $15 at Kelly's to $25 (plus royalties) at the music publishing house.[5]

Waterson & Synder and most other music publishers made West 28th Street the center for promoting popular music. A journalist, Monroe Rosenfeld, walking along and hearing the clutter of dozen of voices and pianos, called the discord Tin Pan Alley. The music publishing business was dominated by Jews. Among the oldest and most successful firms was M. Witmark and Sons, founded in 1886. Marcus Witmark (an officer in the Confederate Army) left Georgia for New York City. His three sons (Isidore, Julius and Jay) convinced their father that music publishing was the opportunity for the future. Thirteen-year-old Julius had performed with a minstrel company in New York City. "Julie" was advertised as the "wonderful boy soprano."

Before the Witmark family opened their new publishing venture, Isidore (age 17) sold several of his original songs to other firms. The Witmark firm was the first to transform front-page stories into best-selling songs. They acted on a rumor that President Grover Cleveland planned to marry in the White House.

Isidore Witmark wrote a wedding march for the President, hoping the rumor proved true. The music was already printed when the White House announced the ceremony. The Witmark's keen sense of what the public will buy made their firm among the largest and most profitable. During the 1890s, Witmark consistently published hit songs, with When You Were Sweet Sixteen at the top of the list.[6]

A Jewish composer from Milwaukee, Charles K. Harris, submitted his first song to Witmark. When he received a royalty check for 85 cents, he started his own publishing firm. Harris was the first to sell more than two million copies (After the Ball), and owned the copyright to "a gold mine" as sales continued at 25,000 copies per week (totaling five million). Other Jewish firms on Tin Pan Alley included Joseph W. Stern Company and Shapiro & Bernstein. The most prolific composer (before Irving Berlin) was Harry Von Tilzer who worked for Shapiro and Bernstein. Von Tilzer (a Jew from Detroit who adopted a nordic pen-name) later opened a publishing firm. In 1890 Von Tilzer hit the jackpot when his A Bird in a Gilded Cage sold two million copies.

Leo Friedmann had five million copies sold of his Let Me Call You Sweetheart. Gus Edwards (Gustave Edward Simon in his native Germany) wrote In My Merry Oldsmobile and By The Light of The Silvery Moon. Another Jewish immigrant from Europe, Jean Schwartz, composed a three-million seller, Bedelia. Irving Berlin, a Jewish immigrant, spent eight years living on the pennies thrown by saloon patrons for his singing. He knew by heart the most popular melodies, and he knew the names of their Jewish composers.[7]

Now at age 21, Berlin not only survived the Bowery, but he won a place at the center of the music business. Tin Pan Alley had only one criterion: which song makes the most money (for publisher and writer). Berlin learned in the Bowery saloons what ordinary folks want in a song. His formula had one word, simplicity.

His work schedule (self imposed) called for four or five songs per day. He worked only at night, writing lyrics for music composed later by Ted Snyder (Waterson & Snyder). Berlin consigned most of his lyrics to his storage trunk, except for the few he judged worthy for Snyder to set to music. Out of his first year's creative flood, Berlin found mass public resonance with two songs. A chance remark by a vaudeville performer in a barber shop (my wife's gone to the country) led to Berlin's first hit. The song about a husband freed from his wife's restraints—My wife's gone to the country. I'm so glad!—ends with a Hooray! Another verse—she took the children with her—deserved Hooray! Hooray! The song sold 300,000 copies.

Berlin, unhappy at sharing royalties with Snyder, set words to the music of Mendelssohn (not covered by copyright). Entitled That Mesmerizing Mendelssohn Tune, the song sold over a half million copies. Berlin's days of hoarding pennies were gone. He now had more money in royalties than he knew how to spend. In an interview with a newspaper reporter, Berlin lamented that a song may be a hit for weeks or months, but "folks are still singing Swanee River and My Old Kentucky Home. It's something to be known like Stephen Foster."[8]

The same year (1909) he wrote two hits, Berlin further obscured his Jewish roots by composing his first Christmas tune: Christmas Times Seems Years and Years Away. It was a Tin Pan Alley flop. Three decades later Berlin composed the White Christmas that sold more recordings than any other song in half a century.

When Berlin turned 22, the New York World newspaper applauded his achievement as "the most successful songwriter of the year…who had "cleaned up $15,000 in the past year." The World noted only "eighteen months ago he was a singing waiter in Nigger Mike's Pelham Cafe on Pell Street." That year Berlin had 30 songs (mostly duds) in his published portfolio. Although the newspaper photograph showed Berlin in a spiffy business suit, his slight build (five foot six inches) and questioning eyes betrayed his concern for the future.[9]

Anxious that fame and fortune continue in the year ahead, Berlin composed a series of ragtime melodies. Ragtime, by public consensus, meant music originated by blacks with distinctive syncopation (a shift of accent in a composition that occurs when a normally weak beat is stressed). The word, "rag," became a generic term for a wide range of music by blacks (or a way of claiming authenticity by white composers). W.C. Handy, for example, published The Memphis Blues as "A Southern Rag."[10]

Scott Joplin (the black "King of Ragtime Writers") was the best known composer of piano ragtime music. His hit in 1899, Maple Leaf Rag, established his reputation throughout the United States. The rag sold a half-million copies and provided Joplin with a small but steady royalty income for ten years. When Berlin claimed the title, King of Ragtime, he declared "our popular song writers are not Negroes. Many of them are of Russian birth or ancestry. All of them are of pure white blood." According to Berlin, immigrant Jews had a monopoly on black culture. White song writers certainly took credit for the "coon song" craze.[11]

When Berlin, a teenager, roamed the Bowery, America's mania was the "coon song." The minstrel show depended on caricatures of blacks in songs and dances, but the "coon song" transcended the minstrel hall by occupying a place on pianos in saloons and homes. A typical "coon song" exposes its racist nature in the title: Plant a Watermelon on My Grave and Let the Juice Soak Through. Between 1895 and 1905 six hundred "coon songs" (a new song every week) were published by the same firms that issued sentimental ballads (When You Were Sweet Sixteen). "Coon songs," composed by Northern whites, reflected the mood of the country in support of Jim Crow segregation. If the Civil War had as a goal equality for African Americans, then the 1896 Supreme Court decision providing separate but equal public transportation and schools gave the victory to the South.

In the "coon song," white fantasy established a separate world that reinforced the minstrel stereotypes and added new themes of lust, theft and violence. Fictional black men and women told their own stories about gluttony, laziness and lack of pride in their own race. The black voice was in reality the voice of a white man from Tin Pan Alley.

A small number of "coon songs" were written by African Americans. Ernest Hogan and Bert Williams (genuine blacks who performed in blackface make-up) were condemned by the black community for their "coon songs" which justified the denigration of the race. As African Americans who went along with the blackface theatrical convention, Hogan and Williams gained in dollars what they lost in self-respect. One social critic sees Hogan and Williams as master parodists whose blackface masks and "coon songs" were meant to ridicule white men impersonating blacks.

A 1906 "coon song," published by Witmark, recalls the earliest minstrel tune (Coal Black Rose). The new rendition, My Coal Black Lady, implies that only white women can be ladies: "This coal black lady/She is my baby…Her color's shady/But she's a lady/Don't trifle with my coal black lady."

Black sensuality was a theme in the songs about women. Hotfoot Sue (1896) described uninhibited black fun: "Hotfoot, de gal paces de cullud section/Hotfoot, de shinin' light o' my affection/Hotfoot, de one possessor o' my affection/I'se won dat black gal, Hotfoot. ma Sue."

In I'se Got The Warmest Baby Of Them All (1899), sexuality was expressed in terms of body temperature: "You talk about your warm black babies/Say, I'se got one that will make your heart beat fast/And she's right from the state of Alabama/Where all those pretty gals dwell."

Since explicit sexual words by Tin Pan Alley were taboo, the 1904 Make A Fuss Over Me dealt with female sexuality (in a slight subterfuge): "There used to be in Tennessee/A gal in swell society/She loved a coon who couldn't spoon/Altho' he tried from morn 'till noon/At last she sighed, Now man, you've tried/To ask me for to be your bride/You've fussed and fussed, and I'll be cussed/If you keep on my heart will bust/If I'm to be your wife/You'd better come to life/And make a fuss over me."

An 1880 song on black male sexuality lacks any subtle hints and comes directly to the point: "There's a bran new coon in town/He came de other day/A reg'lar la-de-dah/Dat's what de gals all say."

Black male sexuality crosses the "the color line" in the 1905 The Mormon Coon: "I've got a big brunette, and a blond to pet/

I've got 'em short. fat, thin and tall/I've got a Cuban gal, and a Zulu Pal/They come in bunches when I call."

Sexuality displayed by children showed that blacks inherently succumb to their base instincts. Honey, You'se Ma Lady Love, A Coonlet Courtship published in 1897 by Witmark: "Two little piccaninnies sitting on a stile/Billin' and cooing for a very long while/Ole Mammy Jinny came a sneakin' long de fence/Of course dose little niggers didn't have a bit of sense...Dey never saw dat nigger wench she kept right out of sight/She listened to de kissin' on her face it brought a smile/When dese words came from dat stile/Honey, you'se ma lady love."

In America's Victorian era, white society abhorred topics such as sensuality, male potency or pre-marital sex. When such ideas are expressed by "black voices," whites feel justified in maintaining their social distance from African Americans.

Chicken and watermelon (the black man's preferred food from the minstrel show) were other symbols that portrayed uninhibited behavior. I've Got Chicken on the Brain (1899): "There's coons 'round town, they ain't hard to find/Would rather have a pork chop than have their right mind/But I likes my chicken, and I likes 'em fried." My Watermelon Boy (1899) combines food and body lust. "He's a common nigger of a very common kind/And he loves a melon from the heart right to the rind...loves to see him roll up his eyes/When watermelon that boy does spy/No coon can win me, no use to try/Cause I love my watermelon boy."

Black men shun work and have money only when they win at dice. How they spend their winnings is a source of consternation for black women. When a Nigger Makes a Hundred, Ninety-nine Goes on His Back: "I had lots of coons but for your sake/I gave them all the sack/Now you haven't got a dollar, its no wonder that I holler/If a nigger makes a hundred, ninety-nine goes on his back." The black dandy, created in the early days of the minstrel show, reemerged in 1899.

The minstrel show portrayed black men as fun-loving, aimless creatures who had one virtue: they were harmless. Beginning in

1896 the black man revealed a new character. The aimless and harmless man of yesterday became the ominous black slasher, a physical threat to white society. Bully Song (1896): "I's gwine down the street with my ax in my hand/I'm lookin' for that bully and I'll sweep him off dis land/I'm lookin' for dat bully and he must be found/I'll take 'long my razor, I'se gwine to carve him deep/And when I see dat bully, I'll lay him down to sleep."

Razors were the new symbol of black males. The 1900 Leave Your Razors at the Door begins "big burly nigger by de name of Brown/Gave a rag-time reception in dis here town/All his friends and relations with their blades came down/For to mingle in de grand sasshay." An earlier song, Ma Angeline (1896), describes a ball which ends in violence. "Razors got a flyin', Nigs and wenches cryin'/Guns and an' buns an' coons flew in de air...De niggers dey wer' slashin'/Steel dey wer' a clashin'/ Coons were scrapin' all aroun de floor."

The threat of violence by a black man, De Blue Gum Nigger (1899), was meant to arouse fear among whites: "I'se a blue gum nigger/You don't want to fool wid me/I'se as bad a nigger as a nigger man can be." Another man of violence walks the streets. I'm the Toughest, Toughest Coon (1904): "I'm the toughest, toughest coon that walks the street/You may search the wide, wide world, my equal never meet/I got a razor in my boot, I got a gun with which to shoot/I'm the toughest, toughest coon that walks the street."

Frequently, sexual prowess, gambling and violence were compressed into one song. De Swellest Ladies' Coon in Town (1897): "dey all know dat I'm a hot potato/Wid a razor, playing cards, or shooting dice." Not even the black religious leader escapes the stigma of chicken theft and razors. Parson Johnson's Chicken Brigade (1896): "Parson Johnson am our leader/He's de boss old chicken stealer/An' he totes his razor an' he car's a gun/If de chickens dey do run/From de Parson's Chicken Brigade."

The privileges flowing to white Americans simply by being white led to several songs. The best-seller of 1900: "Coon! Coon!

Coon!/I wish my color would fade/Coon! Coon! Coon!/I'd like a different shade/Coon! Coon! Coon! Morning, night and noon/I wish I was a white man!/'Stead of a Coon! Coon! Coon!"

Reversing the 1899 social order, a composer envisioned a "coon" who boasts: "I've got a white man working for me/I'm going to keep him busy you see/Don't care what it costs/I'll stand the loss/It's worth twice the money for to be a boss/Don't you dare to talk 'bout the white 'bove the black/I've got a white man working for me."

In 1900 when European immigrants of earlier decades adopted American values (and new Jewish immigrants became instant Americans), African Americans remained the only permanent aliens. They lacked a national origin which could bestow identity and dignity. In the context of a New York City composed of European immigrants, a composer ridiculed the notion of black identity. Every Nation Has A Flag But The Coon: "I really felt so much ashamed, I wished I could turn white/'Cause all the white folks march'd with banners gay/The Scotch Brigade, each man arrayed/ In new plaid dresses marched to "Auld Lang Syne'/Even Spaniards and Swedes, folks of all kinds and creeds/Had their banners except de coons...Now I'll suggest a flag that ought to win a prize/Just take a flannel shirt and paint it red/Then drew a chicken on it, with two poker dice for eyes/An' have it wavin' razors 'round its head/To make it quaint, you've got paint/A possum, with a pork chop in its teeth."[12]

For M. Witmark & Sons of New York City the "coon song" mania opened a new market among amateurs. In 1905 the firm issued The Witmark Amateur Minstrel Guide and Burnt Cork Encyclopedia. The guide was a sales catalogue offering "everything but your audience." Besides the newer "coon songs" and traditional minstrel tunes, Witmark sold scripts with detailed stage directions. The catalogue listed Crest Burnt Cork (the kind that is used by professionals), tambourines, bones, minstrel wigs, minstrel end collars and minstrel advertising cuts.

Witmark in its catalogue targeted amateur minstrels in "schools, colleges, camps, clubs, lodges and fraternal organizations of all kinds." Witmark's catalogue was not the only source for amateur minstrel shows. The popularity of the amateur productions led Joe Bren of Chicago to a new type of theatrical venture.

Bren recruited the most talented amateurs, gave them a trunk full of materials and sent them off across the country. The clubs, lodges and fraternal organizations that engaged Bren's professional director received a package of services, from stage production to advertising and promotion. The Chicago firm reserved for itself a share of the fund raising from ticket sales. Bren's amateur theatrical venture is known today because it was the catalyst for the radio network minstrels, Amos 'n' Andy.

Charles Correl (Amos) was recruited at an amateur minstrel show sponsored by an Elks Club. Within a few weeks, he was advising groups in the Midwest how to mount an amateur production. He directed shows for the American Legionnaires, Kiwanis, Shriners and church groups. Freeman Gosden (Andy) joined the Bren firm later, and was trained by Correll as a professional director. The two men formed a team and later created a new radio venue in 1926 for blackface (not seen but heard) when white men imitated black dialect. They drew on stock characters from the minstrel show with their caricatures of blacks from the South who migrated to Chicago. Three years later, the NBC radio network hired Correl and Freeman, moving the locale of the show to Harlem. Amos 'n' Andy was the top rated program during the 1930s.[13]

By 1905 vaudeville displaced the professional minstrel show except for Lew Dockstader and a few other traveling troupes. Did amateur groups replace the professionals and reach a larger audience? The question was raised 50 years later. Frank C. Davidson (a 1952 Ph.D., candidate at New York University) compiled a list of publishers who offered minstrel show guides for amateurs. He mailed a survey questionnaire to 19 firms. He heard from 14 publishers, three of which had discontinued amateur minstrel guides in their catalogue.

Seven companies reported a brisk business for the amateur guides, and four wrote "medium." Davidson asked publishers how many orders they filled annually, giving multiple choices (more than 500, more than 300, 100, etc.). The majority of publishers, seven out of 11 sold much more than 500 guides. Davidson asked which types of organzations "stage most minstrel shows today?" Publishers named "Kiwanis, Rotary and similar organizaions" as the most active in the country. Church groups were second on the list for minstrel guides, and high schools ranked third.

If in 1952 amateurs controlled the minstrel stage with as many as 5,000 performances annually, what number could be used for the previous 50 years? How many amateurs blacked up for the stage ritual? In each production the cast varied from 20 to 30 individuals. For the year 1952 at least 100,000 white amateurs performed in minstrel shows. During the first half of the 20th Century, millions of whites took part in a distinctly American secular ritual.[14]

Two years after the amateur minstrel show survey, the U.S. Supreme Court ruled again on the separate but equal rule. In the cold war world of conflict between the United States and totalitarian regimes, the segregation of races in America was an embarrassment (so was the blackface minstrel show).

Irving Berlin in 1909 added his name to the long list of "coon song" writers. As the son of a cantor (and apparently shy with women), Berlin overcame his inhibitions by dramatizing female sexual craving. The woman, of course, was black. Do Your Duty Doctor and Cure My Pain is the plea of Liza Green begging the doctor summoned to her home to cure her "love attack." While the words in the lyrics are not offensive by Tin Pan Alley standards, no one could misunderstand the situation.

"Oh, Oh, Oh, Oh, Doctor, won't you kindly hear my plea?/I know, you know doctor, exactly what is best for me/Hear me sigh, hear me cry; surely you ani't goin' to let me die/For if some love will make me gain/Do your duty doctor, cure my pain."

In another game of words, Berlin wrote Alexander And His Clarinet (1910). In minstrel show tradition, the name Alexander adopted by a player on the stage was as laughable as a white man working for a black man. Alexander visits Eliza in her home where he "played and played like sin." The clarinet works as a sexual symbol. Another of Berlin's black females, Liza Snow, "picked up a book called Romeo," and searched for a man who "sho' could love like a Romeo can." The song's title: Colored Romeo (1910).

Berlin used black dancing as a sign of ecstatic sexuality in the Grizzly Bear (1910): "Hug up close to your baby/Hypnotize me like a wizard/Shake yo'self just like a blizzard/Snug up close to your lady/If they do that dance in heaven/Shoot me hon' tonight at seven."[15]

Most books that deal with Irving Berlin's work delete or disguise his blackface career. In fact, his fascination with blackface covered a span of 34 years, beginning with his "coon song" cycle. Do Your Duty Doctor (1909) was followed by Alexander and His Clarinet (1910), Colored Romeo (1910), Ephraham Played Upon the Piano (1911), When the Midnight Choo Choo Leaves for Alabam (1913), I Want To Be In Dixie (1913), Pullman Porters' Parade (1915), The Minstrel Parade (1916) and A Pair of Ordinary Coons (1916).

Life changed for Irving Berlin in 1918 (age 29) when the draft board sent him to Camp Upton on Long Island. An army training and staging center for troops leaving for France during the First World War, the camp housed many New Yorkers. Army discipline transformed the life-style of the wealthy composer who had relied on a valet and a cook for his daily routine.

Deprived of his usual late morning sleep by the sunrise bugle call, Berlin made an offer to the commander. If he staged a show, using the soldiers at the camp, could he be relived of other duties (especially morning wake-up). The army brass saw an opportunity for themselves in a show used for fund raising. Berlin, promoted to sergeant, assembled a cast and stage crew of 300 men.

Variety (the show business newspaper) reported that the navy has a show (female impersonators exclusively) on Broadway at the Century Theater. Berlin took the article to the camp commander and persuaded him that the army could do better. Relieved of all military duties, Berlin began working at night and sleeping through the morning. Since he could not read or write music, he summoned Harry Ruby from New York City. Ruby, a piano player at a publishing firm, moved to Camp Upton, sharing the barracks with Berlin.

Two songs survived the wartime army's show on Broadway: Oh, How I Hate to Get Up in The Morning and God Bless America. Berlin transformed his anguish over interrupted sleep into the most popular song of the musical revue. His great patriotic song—God Bless America—was discarded by Berlin as too solemn.

Almost 20 years later radio diva Kate Smith introduced the nation's unofficial anthem. Perhaps Berlin's uncertainty about God Bless America in 1918 stemmed from his Jewish outsider's sense of insecurity. After 24 years in the United States Berlin filed a petition for naturalization. One year later in 1918 the court awarded him citizenship.

The World War did not suppress Berlin's obsession with the blackface minstrel show. His army musical production had the traditional minstrel semi-circle, with a cast of hundreds in blackface. He wrote a traditional blackface "love" song (Mandy) that survived for 25 years. He also wrote a "coon song" for the army's show: Ragtime Razor Brigade.

In another act of the army show, Darktown Wedding, the cast in blackface impersonated women in ribbons and curls. A year later Berlin, free of the army, revived the feature song of Darktown Wedding for the Ziegfeld Follies of 1919. The Ziegfeld troupe, identified as "The Follies Pickaninnies," sang Mandy.[16]

Ten years later Berlin wrote the plot and music for a Broadway minstrel show. He could not find finanacial backing for his idea. Instead he sold the story line and music to Warner Brothers for Al Jolson's 1930 film, Mammy.[17]

World War II brought a blackface bonanza to the career of Irving Berlin. Within months after the Japanese bombed Pearl Harbor, Berlin was creating another army show for Broadway (This Is The Army) and supervising his most notable Hollowod film,

Holiday Inn. Produced by Paramount, Holiday Inn became a Hollywood legend when Bing Crosby and Fred Astaire performed together for the first time. The film's title led to a new hotel franchise. Bing Crosby's recording of White Christmas (one of the film's holidays) sold over 25 million copies.

Holiday Inn, a film with an anemic plot, succeeded as a musical smorgasbord. Crosby and Astaire are a song-and-dance team until Crosby decides to forgo vaudeville, retreating to an old country house in Connecticut. His intent is not to abandon show business completely. He converts the old house into a country inn with a stage for musical extravaganzas. The film's gimmick is that performances occur only on holidays, leaving 350 days for Crosby's relaxation.

Before the stage show for Abraham Lincoln's birthday starts, Crosby applies black make-up to the face of Marjorie Reynolds, the female co-star. Seeing actors blacking up was essential to assure the film audience that the cast was really white. The set for Lincoln's birthday was far more elaborate than any other holiday. The camera scans a band (saxophone, trumpet, piano, drums, trombone, violin and banjo), 11 men, all in blackface. A Mississippi paddle boat serves as the backdrop with bales of cotton on the stage. Crosby enters, wearing an old fashioned frock coat, a battered top hat and white gloves. Black makeup envelopes his face, framed by wooly white sideburns that reach to his chin. He sings the holiday tune, entitled Abraham. The high point of the song is the refrain: "Abraham set the darkies free."

When Crosby runs out of steam, the chorus of six females and six males in blackface take up the performing chores. The females wear bizarre costumes with broad argyle patterns on full-length dresses and a white apron embroidered with polka dots. Without the audience hearing a word, the costumes themselves convey black culture as ridiculous. The female co-star, Marjorie Reynolds, enters to sing her part. She wears blackface, a shorter striped dress and white bloomers. Her hair is arranged in pigtails (about six or seven) sprouting from her head.[18]

As filming of Holiday Inn concluded, Berlin telephoned General George Marshall, the U.S. Army's chief of staff, offering his musical know-how for an army show on Broadway. Marshall, aware of Berlin's success in 1918, approved diverting 350 soldiers from training in order to produce This is The Army. The 1942 army show was preserved in a film issued by Warner Brothers in 1943.

In the first frame of the film, the audience learns the anticipated extravaganza is "Irving Berlin's This is The Army." The stage show and movie version express Berlin's ideas about Amercian society and how the army reflects our values. Berlin's ego (he sings his old hit, Oh How I Hate to Get Up in The Morning) and the role of blacks propels the film.

When Berlin wrote Oh, Oh Doctor Cure my Pain in 1909, he revived a minstrel tradition. The licentious black female originated in the 1830s with Coal Black Rose. For his 1942 worldview, the black woman is sanitized. Blackface Mandy, who causes frentic arousal, insists on marriage before any love making.

A major production in the film, Mandy has a seated chorus of 80 men (white soldiers in uniform) and 19 blackface singers and dancers. The six "women" in blackface are really men in feminine costumes. The blackface males all wear zoot suits (somewhat shorter coat and less baggy pants for tap dancing). The zoot suit (in Berlin's eyes) was Harlem's unofficial uniform.

The zoot suit fad started with black musicians in 1941, and lasted about three years in New York City and Los Angeles. In the Autobiography of Malcolm X, the zoot suit represented a threat to the white establishment. When Malcolm, living in Harlem, answered his summons for the draft board in 1943, he wore his most outlandish zoot suit and spoke only in jive jargon. He was rejected as unfit for military duty. The zoot suit ploy worked for Malcolm and it also worked for Berlin.

Mandy, as song and dance, is a minstrel number of the past. In order to connect the blackface performers to the real time of 1943 (and to current black culture), the zoot suit costumes carried a powerful visual message of black separation from white American culture.[19]

Alexander's Ragtime Band introduced Berlin to an international audience in 1911. He took credit for transforming black music into a fad for white audiences. Alexander, as the musical maestro, leads a bouncy marching band rather than a syncopating ragtime group. But the word ragtime in the title convinced whites that Berlin had a unique access to black culture. He appropriated the words associated with black dancing and exploited white fascination with "coon songs." During the 1930s Berlin's music matured as it reached for a sophisticated audience on Broadway with As Thousands Cheer (1933).

At the height of his fame he reverted to the insecure immigrant who had to prove his whiteness. Married to a Roman Catholic, Berlin professed no commitment to either Judaism or Christianity. During the 1930s the cornerstone of German nationalism was the hated of the vile Jews. Just prior to America's entry into World War II, anti-semitism had infected the nation through the fiery speeches of Gerald L.K. Smith and Father Coughlin.[20]

Berlin, always the son of a cantor and an immigrant from Russia, could not escape the tide of resentment against Jews. He reacted by making the minstrel show the centerpiece for two Hollywood films. Through This is The Army and Holiday Inn, he fashioned an all inclusive umbrella of American whiteness.

GERSHWIN'S RACIAL PROFILING

Warner Brothers in 1945 produced a musical biography of George Gershwin, a cherished Hollywood icon. Though he died in 1937, the film version of his life, Rhapsody in Blue, has a permanent place on video shelves to this day. Hollywood wanted to do even more to immortalize Gershwin. At the opening of the 1984 Olympic Games in Los Angeles, 84 grand pianos appeared on a lavish outdoor stage. When 84 pianists played Rhapsody in Blue in unison, Los Angeles transformed an American song writer into a world-class composer.[1]

The 1945 film, in spite of trite dialogue and omission of George's brother and sister, is the best representation of Gershwin's life and musical works. The several books about his life do not reproduce the sound of his music (which above all is the meaning of his existence). In a more recent film documentary, Gershwin Remembered, nearly half of the scenes came from Hollywood's Rhapsody in Blue.[2]

The word "Jewish" is never spoken in the 1945 film biography. Yet, the Gershwin family was Jewish, George's friends were Jewish, George's music colleagues were Jewish and he lived within the world's largest Jewish community (New York City).

The film makers avoided the word Jewish and substituted the word American. During the film's moments of tension or conflict, characters describe George: "You can give America a voice...George is an American. He writes of America for America...He will write American music, but great music. Mr. Gershwin leading the way to a new musical expression that is typically American...You are

America personified...He gave voice to the America he knew and loved so well."

Ambivalent about their own Jewishness, Warner Brothers cast Gershwin in their own image of 100 percent American. There were hints that revealed to the Jews in the audience that George was the son of (Jewish) immigrants, living in a Second Avenue (Jewish) neighborhood. His parents (Rosemary DeCamp spoke with a very slight accent) sounded like immigrants, but everyone else in the neighborhood had standard American diction.

The Gershwin family was solidly middle class, supported by father Morris' succession of businesses—bakeries, restaurants and Turkish baths. For mother Rose a piano in the parlor was an essential sign of middle-class status. George's musical career starts at age 12 when the mother decides that Ira (the eldest son) should have lessons on the new piano. George, completely surprising the family, shows off his piano playing skills. On his own George had used player pianos in the neighborhood to learn technique. He was so proficient with the piano roll sound that he later made hundreds of music rolls.

For the next three years, the family piano belonged only to George, as he progressed from piano novice to master. Outgrowing several neighborhood music teachers, George finally had lessons with Charles Hambitzer who had a studio near Columbia University. Hambitzer, a musical prodigy, had mastered the piano, violin and cello. He performed in New York, giving piano recitals and playing the violin with orchestras. Besides teaching and performing, Hambitzer had a contract with the Schuberts to compose musicals. Gershwin said, Hambitzer was "the first great musical influence in my life."

While practicing the works of Liszt, Chopin and Debussy, Gershwin discovered the popular music of Jerome Kern and Irving Berlin. Against the advice of Hambitzer, Gershwin quit high school and found a job as a song plugger with Jerome H. Remick & Company. At age 15, he was the youngest piano pounder in Tin Pan Alley.

Promoting the music of others did not suit Gershwin. He wrote a dozen songs, but sold only one. After three years at Remick's, Gershwin left for a creative job as staff composer at T.B. Harms Publishing Company. Max Dreyfus, who ran the company, encouraged Gershwin to perform with Nora Bayes, a leading vaudeville star. She had selected two of his songs for her repertoire.

Just a year later (1919), Gershwin met Irving Berlin at Harms Music Company. Berlin played a song which Max Dreyfus agreed to publish. Since Berlin could not transcribe music, Gershwin was asked to do the job. After committing Berlin's work to paper, Gershwin worked out an original arrangement which he played for Berlin. "It was so good, I hardly recognized it," Berlin said. Gershwin then proposed that he serve as Berlin's full-time musical secretary. Berlin declined.[3]

Gershwin had developed as a song writer under the influence of Berlin, especially his popular ragtime and "coon songs," such as A Pair of Ordinary Coons (1916). Gershwin struck out with Berlin in 1919, but his fateful meeting with Al Jolson later that year proved a turning point in his career.

His publisher, T.B. Harms, had tried to promote a Gershwin song called Swanee with little success. Then at a party in honor of Al Jolson, Gershwin played the piano for the entertainment of the guests. He played his Swanee which caught the attention of Jolson. With much enthusiasm, Jolson promised to add the song to his Broadway revue (Sinbad). Jolson's endorsement and his photograph (in whiteface) on the cover of the sheet music made George Gershwin famous. Within a few months, Swanee became a best seller, earning for Gershwin the most money in royalties during his lifetime.[4]

Swanee has invigorating music with hack lyrics (repeating such phrases as old folks at home, my mammy watching for me, and D-i-x-i-e). The real Al Jolson sang Swanee in the 1945 Gershwin film. This was his final appearance in a Hollywood motion picture. A year later in the Jolson Story, Jolson is the hidden voice behind the face of Larry Parks.

Fame gave George Gershwin the opportunity to write all the
music for George White's Scandals of 1920. He stayed with the
Scandals for the next four years, publishing 34 songs. During the
1922 Scandals, Gershwin wrote a 20-minute opera, Blue Monday.
George White dropped the opera (performed by whites in blackface)
after the first night. In the 1945 film the 20-minute opera,
condensed to five minutes, has a cast of about 20 men and women
who strut and sway to the tempo of a barroom piano. Gaudy
costumes identify the men as black dandies (recall the song: When
a Nigger Makes a Hundred, Ninety-Nine Goes on His Back).

Vi, the female protagonist, appears in the bar. She sings Has
One of You Seen Joe (her lover). She wears a flamboyant outfit
that matches the black dandies. Her costume is that of a black
prostitute, with her skirt of bold stripes, split from hip to ankle,
revealing a shapely thigh. In this scene of the underside of black
life, Joe must be a pimp.

When Joe finally arrives, his woman Vi professes her love for
him. Meanwhile, a telegram delivered to Joe in the baroom arouses
Vi's jealousy. She, inferring that the message is from another woman,
grabs a knife and plunges it into Joe's back. He stumbles to a chair,
showing her the telegram (which is about his mother). Singing in
rich baritone notes Joe proclaims "I'm Going To See My Mother."
He dies on the barroom floor. It was all a tragic misunderstanding.
The operatic quality of the voice solos do not erase the black cartoon characters.

Gershwin, like many New York City whites, traveled uptown
to Harlem for the excitement of black music and dance. Some
selected whites were invited to private parties in Harlem. Gershwin
became a Harlem regular, often in the company of Carl Van Vechten,
an aficionado of the black life-style and an important music critic.
Van Vechten authored his tribute to Harlem with the book, Nigger
Heaven. At the time, 1926, the book was a sensation because it
claimed to document life in Harlem by a sympathic white writer.[5]

For Gershwin and Van Vetchen, who both absored from early
childhood the "coon song" images (prodigy of the minstrel show),

no visits to Harlem nightclubs could erase their African American archetypes. Through the lens of white culture, black men were overly-dressed pimps, women were sluts or whores until they turned into stout Aunt Jemimas. Frequently the pimp was also the dice man and the snow man. Van Vechten included at the end of his novel a "Glossary of Negro Words and Phrases." Snow and happy dust translated into cocaine.

Van Vetchen's narrative is within the minds of the black characters who conveniently express the author's point of view. Mary, a black character who was too civilized (enjoying Schubert and Schumann), exclaims: "Savages! Savages at heart! And she had lost or forfeited her birthright, this primitive birthright...a birthright that all the civilized races were struggling to get back to...To be sure, she, too, felt this African beat—it completely aroused her emotionally—this love of drums, of exciting rhythms...this warm, sexual emotion."[6]

Just as Van Vetchen portrayed blacks as primitives ruled by their sensual impulses, Gershwin gave operatic voice and music to his image of black culture. Gershwin's "coon song" arias failed, however, to win over music critics. "Blue Monday Blues," wrote a New York World writer, "was the most dismal, stupid and incredible blackface sketch that has probably ever been perpetrated. In it a dusky soprano finally killed her gambling man. She should have shot all her associates and turned the pistol on herself."[7]

When Gershwin's Blue Monday played for one performance at the 1922 Scandals, Paul Whiteman led the orchestra. He decided that the future of music belonged to "Jazz," and he sponsored "An Experiment in Modern Music," in February, 1924. Irving Berlin and Geoge Gershwin (and others) were asked to submit new compositions. Berlin backed out, but Gershwin inspired by the challenge wrote his entry in less than a month. Whiteman had convinced the white journalists that he was pioneering the new American jazz. Actually, James Reese Europe and the Clef Club Symphony Orchestra of Harlem performed at Carnegie Hall in 1912. Europe and his orchestra "astounded the white critics and public who had not yet become acquainted with the sound of syncopated music or 'jazz.'"[8]

Gershwin, playing his Rhapsody in Blue with Paul Whiteman's Orchestra, had the greatest triumph of his career at Aeolian Hall in New York City. The performance was sold-out due to Whiteman's shrewd self-promotion. The audience lavished applause and cheers on the 26-year-old Gershwin. In previous decades the code words for black music were ragtime and jazz, but Gershwin used the term blue in the title of his work. Was black culture at the heart of the composition?

In an interview, Gershwin described the Rhapsody in Blue as his effort "to express our manner of living, the tempo of our modern life with its speed and chaos and vitality." He makes no mention of specific inluences from black music. Instead he says, "composers assimilate influences and suggestions from various sources."[9]

Michael Tilson Thomas, a conductor who favors Gershwin's music, recognizes "an evocative quality, you always know its a Gershwin piece." The longing quality was, for Thomas, a synthesis of Jewish and black music. Academic critics in 1924, such as Daniel Mason of Columbia University and Edward Hill at Harvard, wrote that Rhapsody in Blue was too Jewish, "a menace to our artistic integrity." The music world, "especially in New York, is dominated by Jewish tastes, with their oriental extravagance, their sensuous brilliancy."[10]

George Gershwin and his family were never conspicuously "too Jewish." They transformed themselves from typical immigrant Jews to assimilated Americans. The eldest son, Ira, was named Israel on the birth certificate in 1896 (a year earlier his parents arrived from Russia). George's birth certificate read Jacob. The father's name changed from Moishe Gershovitz to Morris Gershwin.

When Ira turned 13 in 1909, the family gave him a fancy bar mitzvah in a kosher restaurant, attended by 200 guests. Two years later the Gershwin family neglected any religious ritual for George. Between 1909 and 1930, the Gershwin family made their way in New York City without a rabbi or synagogue.[11]

Frances Gershwin, the family's only daughter, wanted to marry a young violinist, Leopold Godowsky, Jr. Mother Rose said the young man would never amount to anything, always in the shadow of his father. Leopold Godowsky, Sr., was the outstanding pianist of his time. Frances and Leopold in spite of the mother's objections decided on a "surprise marriage" in the penthouse apartment of Ira Gershwin.

A friendly judge provided a marriage license just 24 hours before the ceremony. On the day of the wedding, a jeweler in his car brought wedding rings to the corner of Broadway and 103rd Street where Frances made her selection. The final hurdle for the young couple was finding a rabbi. Using a directory the Gershwins looked for a rabbi who lived nearby (the wedding had to take place precisely at four because the parents and George had six o'clock train reservations). Ira called a rabbi who recognized the Gershwin name and happily accepted the assignment.[12]

Seven years later another rabbi officiated at George's funeral service in Temple Emanu-El on Fifth Avenue in New York City. The Gershwins had a Jewish identity, but no pattern of religious observance. Like many Jews at the turn of the century who immigrated to the United States, the Gershwins wanted to be Americans. But the Christian community viewed Jews as a separate race, as well as a separate culture. For Christians a Jew is a Jew, regardless of life-style.

The success of Gershwin's Rhapsody in Blue led Time to feature Gershwin in the magazine. Time bestowed on Gershwin the honor of its first cover for a composer. In describing Gershwin as "a young Jew," Time editors thought little about such a label. A Jew is a Jew. The article went on to define "composer George Gershin, famed jazzbo, had recently returned from Europe...had finished the piano concerto which Dr. Walter Damrosch had commissioned him to write for the New York Symphony Orchestra."[13]

While Gershwin knew the distinctions between orthodox religious Jews and secular Jews, he also knew that no such distinctions mattered much in the Christian view. During the 1920s Gershwin visited Florida where signs on the beaches warned: "No Jews or Dogs Allowed." When he traveled to Lake Placid in New York, he was denied admission to the Lake Placid Club because he was a Jew.

Anti-Semitism in the United States was a reality that Jews lived with during the 1920s. Then in 1933, the new German government under Adolph Hitler began a campaign that imposed on Jews the status of outsider (no work, no schooling and no businesses). On March 21, 1933, The New York Times reported: "Nazis Hunt Arms in Einstein Home, Only a Bread Knife Rewards Brown Shirts' Search for Alleged Huge Cache, Ousting of Jews Goes On, Physicians Are Removed From Hospitals and Judges From the Criminal Courts, Bruno Walter Departs, Philharmonic Conductor Cancels Frankfort Concert."[14]

Gershwin, who had visited Paris, Vienna and Berlin several years before, heard an eyewitness account of events in Germany from Leopold Godowsky, Sr. Godowsky and composer Roger Sessions, on their return from Europe, gave an interview to The New York Times in June, 1933.

Sessions "said there was not an opera house in Germany that had not been adversely affected by the ousting of Jewish conductors and musicians...after the burning of the Reichstag he had witnessed beatings of Jews in the streets by brown-shirted mobs."

Godowsky, in an ominous prediction, told The New York Times that "the fierce Hitlerites revealed (their) brutal coarseness and violence. The natural Teutonic hatred of the Jews had full outlet, as the German is nothing if not thorough. You can imagine the consequences."[15]

As Hitler attacked the Jews in Germany beginning in 1933, Father Charles Coughlin gained a wide audience for his radio broadcasts in which he blamed the Jews for all the economic and social woes in America. Father Coughlin, a Roman Catholic priest from Royal Oak, Michigan, made his first attack against the Jews in a radio broadcast in February, 1930. He continued his anti-Semitic diatribe for the next 12 years, reaching an audience of millions from New York to California.[16]

Jewishness in America during the 1930s was a liability that most Jews concealed, The Gershwin family's Jewishness played out among themselves in the annual Passover dinner, the homemade pickled herring and the Yiddish bon mot. George once even thought of writing a Jewish opera, based on The Dybbuk written in Yiddish by S.S. Ansky. The plot concerns a young man who pursues the mysteries of the Kabbalah. Like King Tut's tomb, the Kabbalah carried a curse for those forbidden to pry into its esoteric knowledge. Sure enough, the young man dies, but his soul enters the body of his sweetheart who must undergo exorcism.[17]

Gershwin's musical notebook for The Dybbuk included Hassidic dances and Yiddish folk tunes. He scuttled the opera when production rights were disputed. A Jewish opera would have been out-of-character for the man who defined himself as an American (in Paris, Vienna and New York). He did later find an American story in a book by DuBose Heyward, a white poet and first-time novelist from Charleston, South Carolina. The book's plot unfolds among the poorest blacks in Charleston who were addicted to gambling and happy dust.

Unfortunately, Al Jolson also wanted the rights to the Heyward novel for a blackface Broadway musical. Heyward had the choice of selling the music rights to either Jolson or Gershwin. When Gershwin learned of Jolson's interest he wrote to Heyward, "I think it is very interesting that Jolson would like to play the role of Porgy, but I really don't know how he would be in it...The sort of thing I have in mind is a much more serious thing than Jolson can ever do." Jolson dropped his bid when he had trouble finding a composer.[18]

As a work of fiction, Porgy has imagined black characters. One character, however, was an actual person known by many in Charleston as "goat Sammy," the crippled beggar. Heyward's inspiration for his story began with a news article in the Charleston News and Courier. "Samuel Smalls, who is a cripple and is familiar to King Street, with his goat and cart, was held for the June term of Court of Sessions on an aggravated assault charge...he attempted to shoot

Maggie Barnes. His shots were wide of the mark...Smalls had attempted to escape in his wagon and was run down and captured by the police patrol."

Heyward's first words after reading the newspaper item were "just think of that old wreck having enough manhood to do a thing like that." The motive for the shooting, by Heyward's reckoning, originated in sexual passion and jealousy. Even a crippled beggar in a goat cart has a hidden life of desire. Heyward also noted that "it was one of those tragedies on the razor edge of comedy."[19]

Heyward's reaction to the crippled beggar's tale may have hinged on his own bout with polio when he was a teenager. Having lost the use of his right hand, Heyward avoided romantic relationships. He was 38 years-old when he met his future wife. A descendent of an aristocratic family (Thomas Heyward signed the Constitution), the Heyward family legacy evaporated when the father died (DuBose was two). When Heyward's mother died seven years later, he was cared for by an aunt. Polio forced him to drop out of school when he was 16. He spent all of his time reading while other boys played sports. As an adult, Heyward opened a modest insurance agency in Charleston. His time and thought went to the writing of poetry, and in 1922 his first collection of verse, Carolina Chansons, was published.

Heyward's writing style of elevated language and poetic metaphors alters a comedy plot (as envisioned by Al Jolson for Broadway) into a tragic opera for George Gershwin. With the upmost of sincerity, Heyward wrote, "To Smalls I make acknowledgment of my obligation. From contemplation of his real and deeply moving tragedy sprang Porgy...and upon whom I could impose my own white man's conception of a summer of aspiration, devotion, and heartbreak across the color wall."[20]

Heyward set the tone for the novel by a poem preceding the first chapter. "Porgy, Maria and Bess/ Robbins, and Peter, and Crown/Life was a three-stringed harp/Brought from the woods to town/Marvelous tunes you rang/From passion, and death, and birth." The obvious earnestness of the author helped persuade book reviewers in the North that his portrait of black life in the South was authentic. The New York Times review helped make the book a best-seller. "Although it is a matter for wonder that Mr. Heyward has seemed to have gotten inside his characters and their surrounding, it is cause for rejoicing that he has communicated these things he has found to the reader."[21]

The real Porgy inspired Heyward to search within himself for the other characters of his book. Even a sympathic Southerner like Heyward could not pierce "the color wall" for an objective portrait of black life in Charleston. Each of Heyward's major imagined characters—Bess, Crown and Sportin' Life—have a long history in the minstrel show and "coon songs." Whites were victims of black stereotypes along with African Americans. For DuBose Heyward and George Gershwin, the fictional Bess, Crown and Sportin' Life rang true as characters long rooted in American culture.

Heyward wrote the libretto for the Gershwin opera, as well as the novel. Both versions have the same characters and stick to a similar plot line. The characters live in a building complex in which all doors open to an inner courtyard. Catfish Row is a separate world isolated from the sensibilities of white Charleston. Heyward showed no awareness about the role of coercive white power in the 1920s. Instead he portrayed white kindness by gifts of food and coins to Porgy, and a white lawyer saving a black client from jail. The miserable lives of the residents of Catfish Row grew out of alcoholism, adultery, drugs, gambling and black on black violence.[22]

Returning to Catfish Row after a day of begging on the streets, Porgy lifts himself out of the goat cart and joins a crap game in progress. Then Crown and Bess walk into the courtyard. Bess who lives with Crown watches from the sidelines, as Crown, a hulking stevedore, makes a place for himself in the circle of gamblers. Crown argues with one of players, and in a drunken rage kills the man with a cotton hook. Everyone in the courtyard flees to their rooms. Crown, now a murderer, must escape from Charleston. Bess is the only one in the courtyard. She doesn't want the police to find her in Crown's rooms, so she goes from door to door for asylum. The residents of Catfish Row reject her, except for Porgy who holds out his hand and closes his door behind her.

About a month after the killing, Bess and Porgy have settled into domestic tranquility, with the blessings of their neighbors. A black lawyer, Simon Frasier, calls on Bess and Porgy, telling them about the need for a divorce (from Crown) before the two can live together. Porgy asks, "How much dat t'ing cost?" Frasier sets the fee at one dollar. As the lawyer fills out a document, Bess mentions that she never married Crown. Frasier says, "Ah, dat's a complication," and ups the fee to a dollar and a half. Porgy counts out the money from a handful of coins. This scene, a product of Heyward's "creative imagination," comes right out of the minstrel show which ridiculed blacks for appalling ignorance.

The grand parade and picnic of "The Sons and Daughters of Repent Ye Saith the Lord" transforms everyone in Catfish Row. The parade route leads to the wharf where an excursion boat transports the celebrants to Kitiwah Island. Before the boat departs, a wagon-load of watermelons is stored on board for the picnic. During the parade and on the boat, "blue-black feet shuffled and danced." Heyward paints a vivid picture of pagans unfettered by civilization who are "exotic as the Congo...abandon themselves utterly to the wild joy."[23]

Porgy never went on the boat to the festive picnic. Yet, he urges Bess to go along and enjoy herself. As the women prepare the food in a clearing on the island, Bess offers to cut palmetto leaves for tablecloths. When she enters the thick cluster of vines and palms, Bess hears the deep breath of desire before she actually sees Crown. Bess explains to Crown that she has "change my way." But Crown with his "hot hands" overcomes her resolve of fidelity for Porgy.

At nightfall the picnickers leave on the boat without Bess. Most of the Catfish Row residents suspected that Crown fled to the island and that on the day of the picnic he enticed Bess to stay with him. A day later Bess returns to Catfish Row. Porgy pretends nothing has happened. Within a few days, a rumor spreads that "de stevedore is comin' back."

Ending his silence about Crown, Porgy asks Bess if she intends "tou go wid Crown," She answers that "I run tuh he like water," when his hot hands touch her body. She begs Porgy to stop Crown from handling her. He consoles her by saying what kind of a nigger "yuh gots anyway." That night Crown, knife in hand, prows the courtyard, looking for Porgy's door. At the moment Crown eases open the door, Porgy grabs Crown's right wrist and turns the knife on Crown. As Crown lays dead in the courtyard, Porgy laughs and tells Bess "yo' got a man now."

The police learn nothing from the residents of Catfish Row. Since Crown was a fugitive wanted for murder the officers merely requested that Porgy make an identification at the morgue. Petrified that he must look at Crown's face, Porgy is dragged out. His superstitious fear of the dead (expecially a spirit that could seek revenge) makes Porgy choose jail rather than identify Crown.

Meanwhile, Bess under the influence of Sportin' Life, the Catfish Row drug dealer and pimp, agrees to go to New York City. (In the novel Bess leaves for Savannah.) When Porgy serves his sentence for contempt of court and returns to Catfish Row, the women plead with him to forget about Bess. Porgy wants to know where she went. They tell him New York. He asks, "where dat?" The women say it's way up north. Porgy, hitching his goat, vows to find her. Porgy and the goat cart exit the stage as the audience hears "oh Lawd, I'm on my way." So ends the opera.

The character of Bess is as old as the circus origins of blackface clowns who sang Coal Black Rose. In 1833, Thomas D. Rice included the Coal Black Rose character in his Ethiopian opera, Oh, Hush! or, The Virginny Cupids. Two decades later, George White (White's Serenaders) performed a new version of the opera at Barnum's Museum in New York City. In White's "operatic olio," the cast of characters include Dinah Rose, Sambo Johnson and Cuff. Sambo and Cuff (who like Crown and Porgy) vie for the affection of Rose (Bess) who in turn plays one man against the other.

Rose has two men in her home. Each in a different room. She's in the room with Sambo who professes his love: "I wish I was a glove, Rose, upon dat lubly hand/I'd be de happiest nigger ob all in dis land/ My bosom am so full ob lob—'twould soon find some relief/when you took de glove to wipe your nose instead ob a handkerchief." Rose, fully aware of Cuff in another room, says: "My love is strong, and of it's strength dar's none but you can tell."

Cuff, hearing the romantic words between Sambo and Rose, tries to grab a gun from a shelve that has a flour container which spills over his face. Sambo, confronting the white face interloper, demands: "Tell me, you saucy nigger, how you do on dat shelf?" Rose intercedes between Sambo and Cuff, saying that Cuff "he's noffin's else but trash." Figuring out that Rose had hoodwinked him, Sambo questions her: "Is dis your constancy, Miss Rose, you tell me ob all day?"

Sambo turns to Cuff: "Be off, you common nigger!" Cuff replies: "Not until we hab a fight/And, Rose, don't you interfere. I'll show dis moke a sight."/ Rose screams: "Fire! help! murder, suicide, all sorts ob death!"[24]

Neither Bess nor Rose can be constant in a relationship with one man. When Crown flees Catfish Row after the killing, Bess goes to Porgy's door and slips into his room and his bed. Rose, even more brazen, entertains two men in different rooms at the same time. Black women convey dual messages for the white men in the audience of Ethiopian operas. Promiscuous black women undermine the traditional values of family and Christian civilization. The same black women also fulfill the fantasy life of white men. Heyward (handicapped and a long-time bachelor) in his novel of black life elevated his own sexual fantasy to a lyrical description of black primitivism.

From the beginning, the minstrel show portrayed the primitive nature of blacks through ecstatic dancing in an outdoor (plantation) setting. Christianity rooted out the European pagan culture, now

only a legend from the woodland ecstasy cult of Dionysus. Heyward
infused the old blackface stereotypes with a contemporary (1920s)
celebration of primitive abandon. Murder, as well as sexuality, flows
naturally from subterranean passions.

Two decades of "coon songs" infected the minds of Heyward's
generation. When Heyward was 24-years-old, Irving Berlin published his female "coon song," Do Your Duty Doctor (cure my
love attack). Popular ditties ignore education and class divisions.
Everyone, top to bottom in white society, hums the same tune
when it confirms fundamental beliefs about race.

Black female sexuality is the repeated theme of songs, such as
Make a Fuss Over Me (show me how I arouse you): "Ain't it easy
to see/I've an itching to be/siting right on your knee/that's my one
longing plea/if we're goin' to agree/and you want me to love you/
make a fuss over me."

Another major character, Sportin' Life, in Heyward's novel
epitomizes the "coon song," When a Nigger Makes a Hundred,
Ninety nine Goes on His Back. The black dandy from the North
existed side by side with the Southern plantation darky as stock
characters in minstrel shows. Heyward defined the black characters as magical primitives, but he made Sportin' Life an outsider
from New York. Dressed in yellow spats, sky-blue pants and a
scarlet tie displaying a diamond studded horseshoe, Sportin' Life
is the only "octoroon" in Catfish Row. By definition an "octoroon"
is someone with one-eighth black ancestry.

The pure black characters of Catfish Row live by their instincts. Sportin' Life, the octoroon, calculates every word and every gesture in order to entice women into prostitution and drug
addiction. If Porgy is a tragic hero, according to Heyward, then
Sportin' Life is a devilish Northern dandy. Early in the novel, Crown
and Bess are drug addicts who are supplied by Sportin' Life. When
Bess moves in with Porgy she gives up the "happy dust." Waiting
for his opportunity, Sportin' Life asks Bess to hold out her hand.
Half mystified she complies. Sportin' Life sprinkles white powder
on her palm.

The small measure of powder, Sportin'' Life assures her, isn't enough to hurt a fly. Besides it won't "cos' yer one cent." Bess must decide to keep the sample or turn her palm down. She succumbs to his wily scheme. Sportin' Life "heaved a sigh of relief," as Bess gulps the happy dust. Within minutes, she asks for more. Sportin' Life reminds her that "it don't come cheap."

In the traditional minstrel show, the Northern black dandy strutted on the stage like a peacock. Heyward, in need of a character to churn the plot, conceived an up-to-date black dandy. Sportin' Life is the author's device to take Bess out of Porgy's life. When the police dragged Porgy out of Catfish Row to identify the dead Crown, Bess is uncertain what to do. Sportin' Life seizes the opportunity to ensnare her with an offer of happy dust to chase away "dem lonesome blues." He tells her that Porgy will never look on Crown's face, so the police will lock him up in jail.

Bess asks if Porgy will get out soon. Sportin' Life with calculating self-confidence assures Bess that Porgy will be gone maybe for a year, maybe for two years. With Crown dead and Porgy in jail, there's just Sportin' Life to share Bess' bed. His show of sympathy conceals his intent to turn Bess into a Harlem prostitute. He promises her the high life in New York, the "swellest mansion" and dresses of silk and satins. For a moment Bess resists, calling Sportin' Life a rattlesnake. He then offers her more happy dust. She hesitates before giving in. Sportin' Life and Bess strut off the stage. The minstrel show's archetypal wanton black woman (Coal Black Rose) and the Northern black dandy find their ultimate incarnation in the opera, Porgy and Bess.

Crown, the hulking stevedore, traces his lineage to the "coon song" era from 1894 to 1910 (Heyward was born in 1885). The tough bully celebrated in song made his way onto the amateur minstrel stage after May Irwin made a hit with her Bully Song. She sang in 1896: "Have yo' heard about dat bully dat's come to town/He's round among de niggers a layin' their bodies down/I'm a lookin' for dat bully and he must be found/I'm a Tennessee nigger and I don't allow/No red-eyed river roustabout with me to raise a row/I'm lookin' for dat bully and I'll make him bow.

Much longer than most "coon songs," the Bully Song continues: "I's gwine down the street with my ax in my hand/I"m lookin' for dat bully and I'll sweep him off dis land/I'm lookin' for dat bully and he must be found/I'll take 'long my razor, I'se gwine to carve him deep/And when I see dat bully, I'll lay him down to sleep."

A shorter bully song, De Blue Gum Nigger, appeared in 1899: "I'se a blue gum nigger/you don't want to fool with me/I'se as bad a nigger as a nigger man can be."

Then in 1904 another bully song, I'm the Toughest, Toughest Coon, commanded public attention: "I'm the toughest, toughest coon that walks the street/you may search the wide, wide world, my equal never meet/I got a razor in my boot. I got a gun with which to shoot/I'm the toughest, toughest coon that walks the street."

Heyward portrays Crown as a bully who kills a player in a crap game rather than lose his money. Crown's act sets in motion the story of Porgy and Bess, and his death ends the opera when Bess leaves for New York with Sportin' Life. Other than Porgy (a real crippled begger in Charleston), the major characters come from the imagination of DuBose Heyward. Both Bess and Sportin' Life were minstrel show figures who burrowed into the minds of white audiences since 1843. For Heyward, however, they were as real as the crippled black begger. When George Gershwin read Heyward's novel, he found "the truth" about the life of blacks as defined by the dominant white American culture.

Heyward, the white Southerner, saw the conditions of black life in Charleston in 1924 as a consequence of ignorance, superstition and addiction to drugs and alcohol. He did not consider how legal segregation denied blacks education and employment. Heyward, a kind soul, forgave blacks their lack of refinement. He envied (from a distance) their exotic and primitive life-style.

Gershwin, a second-generation Jewish New Yorker, had a family mandate to become American. When he wrote the music for his 1935 opera, Americans accepted the "natural" social order that isolated blacks. New York City had Harlem, and Charleston had Catfish Row. Gershwin, exquisitely in touch with American culture, agreed totally with Heyward about exotic and primitive black music and dance. He also embraced the negative images of blacks in Heyward's novel.

Following the opening night of Porgy and Bess, the New York critics were stumped by Gershwin calling his work a "folk opera." In a gracious gesture, The New York Times invited Gershwin to explain his thinking about Porgy and Bess. He wrote: "Since the opening of 'Porgy and Bess' I have been asked frequently why it is called a folk opera. The explanation is a simple one. 'Porgy and Bess' is a folk tale. Its people naturally would sing folk music. When I first began work on the music I decided against the use of original (traditional) folk material because I wanted the music to be all of one piece. Therefore I wrote my own spirituals and folksongs. But they are still folk music--and therefore, being in operatic form, 'Porgy and Bess" becomes a folk opera."[25]

In spite of his legalistic reasoning in the newspaper article, Gershwin's facts are wrong. Porgy and Bess did not come out of a traditional black folk tale. It was the product of one white man. The black folk music written by Gershwin was neither "black" or "folk." At the time that Gershwin was composing "my own spirituals," black congregations were singing a new form of spiritual.

Starting in 1921, several black composers extended the traditional church repertoire by adding new songs that blended elements of blues and black jazz. The name spiritual was replaced by gospel. Thomas A. Dorsey, a blues singer with the stage name Georgia Tom, gave up secular music and devoted himself exclusively to gospel. He is considered the "Godfather of Gospel." Between 1932 and 1935 when Gershwin composed Porgy and Bess, Dorsey and Mahalia Jackson traveled the country spreading the new gospel sound.

For the next decades, white audiences believed that the opera truly reflected black life. The word "folk" was dropped from the program notes and replaced by "An American Classic." Gershwin took credit for his contribution to grand opera by infusing "the drama, the humor, the superstition, the religious fervor, the dancing and the irrepressible high spirits of the race."

Indeed the opera audiences were enthusiastic, especially in Europe, during tours of Porgy and Bess between 1952 and 1956. The American State Department selected Porgy and Bess to represent the United States in the opera houses of Berlin, Brussels, London, Milan, Paris, Rome, Vienna and Zurich. What did the State Department hope to accomplish during the early years of the cold war?[26]

By having an all-black cast, the opera provided a chance for African Americans to showcase their musical talents. In one sense, black singers on the stage refuted communist claims that blacks were consigned to the drudge jobs in America. But the characters playing out their lives on stage sent another message to Europeans. White America, even in the South, had compassion for unfortunate blacks corrupted by addictions to alcohol, drugs, gambling and sexuality. The opera was mute about the issues of racism and segregation.

The Soviet Union extended an invitation to the Porgy and Bess producers for performances in Moscow. The ministry of culture offered to pay all the expenses of transport, hotels and food, plus salaries in rubles for the opera troupe. The Soviet agenda had different goals than the U.S. State Department. Black performers on the Moscow stage represented communist solidarity with peoples of color throughout the world. Catfish Row, in the eyes of the Moscow audience, was a true slice of life for the blacks oppressed by white capitalists.

Beginning in 1935, Porgy and Bess caused controversy in America, mostly between black critics and the white music establishment. Then in 1998, on the 100 anniversary of Gershwin's birth, a PBS television documentary gave Porgy and Bess a legitimate site on the cultural landscape. Marshalling the "big guns" of academia as advisors, the University of Michigan produced the definitive judgment on Porgy and Bess. Twenty-nine "experts" evalutated the opera in the film documentary. Five were white and 24 were black.[27]

Most of the black speakers had roles in Porgy and Bess productions from 1935 to 1993. Performers included Cab Calloway, Diahann Carroll, Leontyne Price. Simon Estes and Maya Angelou. The only black person with harsh words was Mary Moubrie who led a black hospital workers strike in Charleston in 1970. By coincidence, the social elite had invited a touring company of Porgy and Bess to celebrate Charleston's "most famous lovers." After the performance, there was a reception "with watermelon balls" for the elite, the few black citizens in the audience and the cast.

The hospital strikers leadership did not object to the opera, as such, but to the black cast who failed to lend any support to the plight of black women demanding pay equal to white nursing aides. Under orders from the governor, the strikers were swept off the streets of Charleston into police wagons.

The very first woman to sing the role of Bess in 1935, Anne Brown (a 21-year-old student from Julliard) said, "When my father saw the premiere of Porgy and Bess, he was very disappointed and sad that Negroes had been pictured in usual cliches, ignorant, dope peddlers and users, criminals. We have had enough of that. Its time to stop." Anne Brown did not say if she agreed or not. Her father's negative view was left hanging in the air. She later praised Gershwin for the beautiful music.

The only other black woman to express concern about the negative images of African Americans was Diahann Carroll, who played Bess in the Hollywood movie version of the opera. She refused a film role, but changed her mind at the urging of her husband. He said exposure in a motion picture would propel her career.

The documentary film's producers also issued a 25-page classroom guide to help teachers and students map the trail of how the opera relates to black culture. On page 24, a panel of advisers includes Harold Cruse. He is identifed as "author of the landmark The Crisis of the Negro Intellectual and professor Emeritus at the University of Michigan's History Dept." In a separate promotional brochure issued before the February 4, 1998 broadcast, a heading reads: "Porgy and Bess: An American Voice Featuring Harold Cruse" (his is the ninth name on the list). The producers obviously expected Cruse to lend his name and reputation to the documentary broadcast.

Had the producers consulted the first person on the panel of advisers, Hollis Alpert, they would have learned that Cruse hated the opera. Alpert, "author of The Life and Times of Porgy and Bess," quotes Cruse on page 291: Porgy and Bess is "the most contradictory cultural symbol ever created in the Western World...should be forever banned by all Negro performers." Had the producers read Cruse's The Crisis of the Negro Intellectual, especially page 103, they would certainly scratch his name off the list. Did Harold Cruse appear before the camera in the studio? Was he cut out of the final version?

There are more critical remarks by blacks in Alpert's book (but not in the film documentary). Duke Ellington said, "The times are here to debunk Gershwin's lampblack Negroisms...the music does not hitch with the mood and spirit of the story. It does not use the Negro musical idiom." A writer for the Baltimore Afro-American declared the opera to be "the most insulting, the most libelous, the most degrading act that could possibly be perpetuated against the Negro people."[28]

Why make a film documentary about Porgy and Bess? How many students listen to opera? Was the film a musical project or an attempt to soften African American attitudes toward Jews? In order to make certain that the film's audience learned that George Gershwin was Jewish, the script weaved that fact into the narrative: "The story matter is about black people in the South written by a Jewish man...Two second-generation Jewish Americans, George and Ira Gershwin created the opera...A Jewish man (Gershwin) from New York wanted to hear us sing."

In the printed classroom guide, cultural historian Lawrence Levine wrote: "Jews were marginalized members of American society at this time, like the inhabitants of Catfish Row. Excluded from most professional and white-collar vocations by their ethnicity and lack of formal education, as were Blacks, many Jews turned to the world of entertainment, particularly popular song and dance."

During the 60-year history of Porgy and Bess (opera stage, motion picture and television broadcast) a fair number of black singers had an opportunity to start or build their careers. Gregg Baker, who sang the role of Crown at the 1985 production of Porgy and Bess at the Metropolitan Opera House, recalled the opening night curtain call. For him and the other black singers who trained for years in conservatories a dream came true. "It was really magic," he said. "You're lucky if you experience that once."

Maya Angelou, who performed in the opera's 1952 European tour, emphasized the "great singers who had so few chances to sing (in other operas)." William Warfield, the leading man in the European touring company, demonstrated how he ("my being a black man I know what to do") sang in a spiritual style. Warfield described his first night in Vienna with press and photographers surrounding the black cast. "It was a glorious arrival," he said. "From then on it was one magnificent experience after another." For Martha Flowers who played Bess, Milan was the highlight of the tour. "La Scala...is the most beautiful opera house in the world," she said. "I will never forget it."[29]

Al Jolson read the Porgy novel as the basis for a blackface burlesque of ignorant and licentious Southern blacks. George Gershwin submerged the cartoon quality of the novel by composing music that transcended the plot and characters. Porgy and Bess expressed his own emotions of sadness and elation in a universal musical language. His early attempts at a Jewish opera were thwarted by his desire to abandon his ethnic identity for that of a white American. What better way than compose an opera about the lives of black people (seen through DuBose Heyward's minstrel show telescope).

JEWS IN BLACKFACE

More than anyone else, Al Jolson made blackface performance a worldwide spectacle when The Jazz Singer opened the age of talking movies in 1927. For the next 20 years he helped resurrect the minstrel show in Hollywood films. The minstrel show flourished in America between 1845 and 1875 as the most popular form of show business. Then for the next 75 years it was the favorite of amateurs who mounted shows for civic and fraternal clubs and in colleges, schools and churches.

The minstrel show, surrounded by an aura of mystery, had a compelling fascination for both performers and audience. George Thatcher, a minstrel star in the 1880s, recalled seeing his first show as a young boy. "I found myself dreaming of minstrels. I would awake with an imaginary tambourine in my hand, and rub my face with my hands to see if I was blacked up...the dream of my life was to speak to a performer."[1]

The story of a modern blackface performer seemed to Harry, Jack and Sam Warner (Warner Brothers in Hollywood) the perfect way to introduce the first talking movie to the world. As immigrants from Poland, the Warner brothers had the extra edge of perception of American culture as seen through Jewish eyes. The brothers understood that the minstrel show was a flashy metaphor for the unity of white Americans (regardless of origin). No playbill for a minstrel show spelled out the social meaning of white men in black facial makeup. It was simple intuition on the part of all.[2]

The movie script for The Jazz Singer is itself an intriguing story. Samson Raphaelson, a Jewish New York writer, was inspired by Jolson's performance on Broadway. Raphaelson said Jolson's "voice reminded him of the chazans (cantors) I'd heard as a boy."

Raphaelson combined the vocal inspiration with the known facts about Jolson's early life to write a play about a blackface performer who happens to be the son of an orthodox cantor. The play had a fair success on Broadway. With a disguise of name and a few other alterations, Al Jolson gets to play himself in the movie version. Jolson is doubly blessed: star of the first talkie and his first film autobiography.[3]

If the Warner brothers saw the minstrel show as a metaphor for the opportunities for Jews (as white men) in America, Al Jolson had the honor of representing to the world the Jewish establishment in Hollywood and Broadway. As a man playing the role of his own life and achievement, Jolson (an immigrant from Lithuania) stood in the shoes of other Jewish immigrants—Lee Shubert of Broadway, George Fox of Fox Studios, Louis B. Meyer of M-G-M and Adolph Zukor of Paramount.[4]

Listen carefully to comedian George Jessel as he told mourners at Al Jolson's funeral, "I must inform you of the great inspiration that Al was to the Jewish people in the last 40 years...(Jolson) told the world that the Jew in America did not have to sing in sorrow, but could shout happily about Dixie...and when he cried 'Mammy,' it was in appreciation, not in lament. Jolson was the happiest portrait that can be painted about an American of the Jewish faith."[5]

Two events shaped Al Jolson's personal life and propelled his public career. The two were his coming to America as an Eastern European Jew and the death of his mother less than a year later.

Jolson was born in Seredzius, Lithuania—a crossroads village of mud paths and log houses. Lithuania was a small country in the Russian empire ruled by the oppressive edicts of the Czar. Jolson's father headed the village's synagogue as rabbi and cantor in the poor Jewish community. When Jolson was four, his father emigrated to America, leaving behind mother Naomi and four children.

The family expected to join father Moshe in several months, but his search for a position took the rabbi from city to city during four years. Meanwhile the family lived on the generosity of the maternal grandfather. Jolson was eight years old when mother Naomi and the children left Seredzius for the United States.[6]

The year of Jolson's birth, 1886, was a turning point in the world's Jewish population. Up to then the greatest Jewish concentration was in Russia and Eastern Europe. A small number of Jews lived in Palestine and less than one percent lived in the United States. Poverty among Jews in Russia and the image of "streets paved with gold" in America fed an exodus. The murder of Jewish men and the rape of Jewish women by bands secretly financed by the government also motivated two million Jews to escape Russia for the United States between 1880 and 1920. (Recall Jessel's words "that the Jew in America did not have to sing in sorrow, but could shout happily about Dixie . . . and when he cried 'Mammy,' it was in appreciation, not in lament.")

Nearly half of the Jewish immigrants stayed in New York City, which by 1910 housed 540,000 on Manhattan's Lower East Side. Jolson's family settled in Washington, D.C., where Rabbi Moshe Yoelson headed the Talmud Torah Congregation. On his own, Jolson changed his given name from Asa to Al. His older brother Hirsh made the change to Harry. Al Jolson's Yiddish accent was muted by his self-conscious Southern dialect.

In less than nine months after settling into a new home and a new way of life, Al Jolson witnessed his mother's death. He had opened her bedroom door when he heard her painful screams. The doctor pushed him out of the room, but not before Jolson saw the agony expressed in his mother's face.

As the youngest son in a Jewish household, Jolson had the love of an adoring mother during the four-year absence of the father. With the death of his wife, and four children to raise, Rabbi Yoelson arranged for a bride from Russia. When the new wife gave birth to a son, Al Jolson's childhood ended. He became a school truant, hanging out with street gangs, and consoling himself at the matinee performances of live stage shows at the Lyceum Theatre.

Biographer Herbert Goldman connects Jolson's signature song, Mammy, with mother Naomi. Her death was an epiphany which dominated his inner life (and helps explain the great emotional appeal and pathos of his singing). The personal tragedy of Al Jolson was the key to his career as a singer. But his life as a Jew was shared with the millions of other Jewish immigrants who had to create a new identity in America.

For Jolson the religious Jew who could be easily recognized—by accent, dress, mannerisms, choice of food—was a throwback to Russia. His father represented the typical stodgy old world religious Jew. Jolson's desirable role models appeared on the stage of the Lyceum Theatre where men danced with style and dressed with flair.

In the film The Jolson Story, an insight to his childhood occurs when he ran away from home, taking a train to nearby Baltimore. With a large Jewish population, Baltimore's Jewish social services could have taken Jolson in hand. But Jolson hid his ethnic identity and went into a Catholic Boy's Home.

The film biography condenses much in Jolson's early life.[7] An important influence on young Al was left out totally. The first time Jolson entered a theater, he and brother Harry skipped school for a matinee at the Lyceum. The star of the show, Al Reeves, so overwhelmed nine-year-old Al Jolson that he knew on that day his future career. Jolson never forgot the performer's bravado or the audience's applause.

Reeves (billed as the World's Greatest Banjoist and Comedian) covered his face in black makeup. He wore a loud plaid double-breasted jacket with two rolls of large white buttons down the front. He had a flower in his jacket lapel, a bow tie and a small hat that covered most of his curly hair. Reeves carried a gold-plated banjo for his finale. Although in the eyes of Jolson he strutted on the stage as an idol, Reeves was no great musical talent. Known as the "most risque comic" in burlesque, Reeves agile tongue turned each phrase so it had a double meaning.[8]

Seven years later, teenage Al Jolson joined Al Reeves' Famous Big Company. He belonged to the team of Master Joelson and Fred Moore. Moore and his wife were the on-the-road guardians, as well as his theatrical mentors. With his childhood idol close enough to touch, Jolson studied Reeves for the nuances of body movement, the timing of punch lines (mostly off color), and the inflections of singing style. Reeves helped give the finishing touches to Jolson's stage education in blackface comedy and song.

Al Jolson's career took a great leap when Lew Dockstader offered him a spot in America's most acclaimed minstrel show. Dockstader's own career was at the peak after two decades in elusive pursuit of fame. In 1886 Dockstader opened a theater in New York City, hoping to revive the glory days of the minstrel show when the Christy Minstrels and the Bryant Minstrels had their names enshrined on Broadway. But the audiences did not show up, and he lost his life savings. The curtain came down as reported in the New York Dramatic Mirror, "Dockstader's Minstrel Hall closed its doors last Friday, owing to the meagre patronage accorded the entertainment, and the minstrels have disbanded for good."[9]

Dockstader had misread the signs of the times. Burlesque (real women in scanty costumes not the blackface female imposters of the minstrel show) and vaudeville (every show had at least one blackface song and dance routine) had replaced the minstrel show in New York City. The demise of the permanent minstrel hall was not the end of the minstrel show. In hundreds of towns along the rail routes, the arrival of the minstrel show was a special event, much like the circus.

After reaching the pinnacle of minstrelsy with his own theater, Lew Dockstader had to take a job with the Primrose and West Minstrels. George Primrose and William West had the best traveling show in the nation. Dockstader's stage talent and management skills were rewarded when West left the company. Dockstader joined in a partnership with Primrose. The troupe traveled under the name of "Primrose and Dockstader." When Primrose had enough of travel in 1903, Dockstader had the company all to himself.

There is proof that the traveling minstrel show made a small fortune for Dockstader. His scrapbook in the Billy Rose Theatre

Collection of the New York Public Library has a newspaper photograph of Dockstader, "the Ebony King," and his Long Island friends in his 1906 Thomas Flyer automobile. That year the auto sold for $6,000 and a nickel bought a loaf of bread.

Dockstader recruited Jolson in 1908 for his traveling minstrel troupe. At that time, if Jolson's circus stint (truant from school) was included, he had at age 22 a resume with ten years of performing experience. In January of 1908 Jolson played the Victory Theatre in San Francisco. His solo vaudeville act billed as "The Blackface with the Grand Opera Voice." Jolson's salary was $125 a week, but the 1908 bookings ended May 2nd in Houston, Texas. Early in April while Jolson played the Majestic and Dockstader the Capital Theatre in Little Rock, the two met and struck a deal. Jolson agreed to work for $75 a week the first season, $100 the second, and $125 thereafter. Dockstader told Jolson $125 was the salary he paid himself.

Jolson's 1908 tour with Dockstader began in August at the Plainfield Theatre in Plainfield, New Jersey. Between August 10, 1908 and December 18, 1909, the minstrel troupe performed in 165 cities. More than half of the performances were for one night, in such cities as Springfield, Illinois and Sioux City, Iowa. In the bigger cities, such as Detroit and Philadelphia, Jolson had time to see the local sights during the afternoons before showtime.[10]

One city, however, was recognized as the minstrel show capital of the United States. At the Globe Theater in Boston, Lew Dockstader's Minstrels sang and cavorted for 19 consecutive days in January of 1909. During Dockstader's stay in Boston, about 30,000 fans cheered on the minstrels.[11]

Seven months into Jolson's 165 city tour, the Dockstader troupe appeared at the Majestic Theatre in Brookyn. Their performances from February 8th to 14th, included an unusual Friday matinee for Lincoln's Birthday. The Brooklyn Eagle carried an announcement about the show on the entertainment page. Surely, Dockstader's press agent wrote the column and gave it to the editor with free tickets. "Minstrelsy of a superior quality unlike anything in black face be will offered by Lew Dockstatder and his company of seventy.... The fun is at a meeting of the Possum Hunt Club, an exclusive colored social organization that sends a colored man to find the North Pole.... and bring it back."[12]

A photograph published in 1980 by the International Al Jolson Society shows the stage set for the Possum Hunt Club with 48 blackface men in riding boots, white breeches, cutaway jackets, white shirts and bow ties. A large tree at the back of the set helps create the outdoor atmosphere of a country club.

An act two photograph shows an African jungle on stage with dozens of tropical trees and a man-size cooking pot in the center. Dockstader, standing in the pot, clasps his hands in prayer, while Jolson on both knees looks fearfully at the cannibals. Jolson and Dockstader wear suits and hats. Everyone else on stage wears jungle costumes of grass or fabric skirts, carry spears and long shields. Jolson and Dockstader are easily identified in the photograph captioned, "Boo-Hoo-Land," a stopover on the parody journey to the North Pole which originated at the Possum Hunt Club.

What the minstrel show meant to America and what it meant to Al Jolson as an immigrant Jew can be revealed in the events of 1908 in Springfield, Illinois. On August 15, 1908, the front page of many newspapers carried similar headlines: "Illinois Mobs, Kill and Burn—Foiled in Attempt to Lynch Two Negroes, Angry Whites Start Destructive Raid—Troops Bring Gatling Gun—Mob Sets Fire to Negro District and Refuses to Allow the Fire Department to Work." A race riot in Springfield seemed impossible. All the nation knew Springfield as Abe Lincoln's hometown.[13]

William Walling, a white writer who came to Springfield from Chicago, covered the riot. In his article, The Race War in the North, he wrote "we have closed our eyes to the whole awful and menacing truth—that a large part of the white population of Lincoln's home...have initiated a permanent warfare with the negro race." The reporter witnessed Springfield's charred black homes and the looted black businesses. He heard, not once, but a dozen times, "Why, the niggers came to think they were as good as we are."[14]

Four days before the riot in Springfield, Al Jolson appeared for the first time in a minstrel show. He had third billing with Lew Dockstader's Minstrels on a tour of 165 cities that started in Plainview, New Jersey, and played in Springfield, Illinois at the Chatterton Opera House on November 2, 1908

Among the hundreds of thousands of Jewish immigrants who came to the United States from Russia to escape anti-Jewish campaigns, a handful settled in Springfield. After the race riot in Springfied, newspapers reported that the mob took care not to disturb "white men's places" of business. Among the few immigrant Jews four owned businesses which were looted. Reuben Fishman who owned a pawnshop told the reporter from the Illinois State Journal that his losses amounted to $3,000. The article quoted Fishman in his broken English, as saying, "I vill now haf to go in der poorhouse."

The comic Jewish parody in the newspaper and the vandalism against Jewish stores signified that Jews were not considered white, but an alien race. Abraham Raymer, a Jewish immigrant from Russia, became Springfield's number one scapegoat. Raymer, a sometime peddler and waiter, as the most recent immigrant was labeled an "anarchist" who plotted the riot to overthrow the Springfield government. The police did obtain one confession from Raymer under brutal interrogation. He admitted an interest in Zionism. Between September and late December, Raymer was the defendant in four trials.

Illinois State Attorney Frank Hatch charged that Raymer was a ringleader in the rioting. At the first trial for murder, Prosecutor William St. Johns Wines told the jury Raymer did not have to assault Donnegan (a black man lynched by the mob), but if he was part of the crowd, "aiding and abetting in the crime," he was guilty. The verdict went against the prosecutor. No one else in Springfield was brought to trial for the murder of Donnegan.[15]

At his second trial for "property damage," Raymer was acquitted. In between the second and third trial of Abraham Raymer, Springfield's Chatterton Opera House presented Lew Dockstader's

Minstrels. George W. Chatterton, the manager, reported to The New York Dramatic Mirror a full house for Dockstader's Minstrels, "Standing Room Only."[16]

In November Raymer stood trial for "rioting," and again the jury said not guilty. At the end of December, Raymer had a fourth and final trial. He was convicted of "petty larceny," and fined $25 plus a sentence of 30 days in jail. Raymer was the only person in Springfield tried in court for any crime related to the riot.

Al Jolson and Abraham Raymer shared the same memory of Jewish life in Eastern Europe defined by violence and poverty. In America the black man, however, was the official outsider. A Jew (even if he could not pass for a white American) automatically escaped the bottom rung of the class system.

Raymer, an uneducated man with no special skills, lived on the margin of a society strange to him. He was the obvious outsider, speaking with a thick accent and wearing ill-fitting clothes. Photos of Jewish peddlers from that period show a man pulling a handcart, wearing baggy clothes, and a shaggy beard which covered his face like a mask. Raymer's Yiddish accent was cause for laughter and ridicule.

Abraham Raymer was not an innocent victim of religious persecution when he stood trial. He was so easy to recognize by the witnesses from the edge of the mob. For those intense hours of the race riot, Raymer was not an outsider. He merged into the mass as a white man, voicing his stake in the struggle for subordination of the black residents of Springfield.

Al Jolson transcended his Eastern European Jewish origins and erased the insecurity of immigrant status by linking himself to the 1843 origins of the blackface minstrel show. Jolson was not a man who read books, but he had an intensive "graduate" course from Lew Dockstader and the other old-time minstrels on the lineage of minstrelsy. Jolson worked, ate and caroused with minstrels who traced their tradition to Daddy Rice, Dan Emmett, Edwin P. Christy, Dan Bryant and George Primrose. Each performance on the tour was a ritual reenactment of the tradition passed from minstrel to minstrel over six decades.

The "Standing Room Only" audience at Springfield's Chatterton Theater presentation of Lew Dockstader's Minstrels wanted assurance that social equality of white and black in America was absurd. The Possum Hunt Club which sent an expedition to bring back "the North Pole" was as ridiculous as "niggers who think they are as good as we are." In Springfield laughter did not preclude violence. Blacks were, after all, no better than their African cannibal forefathers.

Jolson's high ambition, kinetic energy and volatile personality burst the confines of Dockstader's company. As a child he ran away from home, as a performer he skipped out of Dockstader's troupe to star in the rival Wilkerson's Minstrels of Today. Wilkerson's audiences were skimpy and the cast went unpaid. Jolson, tied to Dockstader by a three-year contract, returned to the troupe like a penitent child.

A New York theatrical agent as ambitious as Jolson (and only two years older) signed up Jolson for a summer vaudeville tour during Dockstader's layover. The agent, Arthur Klein, then approached the Shuberts of Broadway to take on Jolson. The Shuberts also managed Dockstader's tours. With a little pressure and after a few theaters in Shubert's circuit failed to attract an audience, Dockstader released Jolson from the contract.[17]

The Shubert brothers (Lee and J.J.) owned 13 theaters in Manhattan, as well as 60 theaters in major cities. The Shuberts also controlled the bookings in hundreds of theaters in the United States. Besides the theater empire, the Shuberts owned 50 dramatic and musical companies that traveled throughout the country. A third brother, Sam, created the theater empire before his death in 1905.

The Shuberts had immigrated from East Prussia to Syracuse, New York. The father came to the United States several years before the other family members. He worked as a peddler. When mother Carrie came to Syracuse with the children, she opened a boarding house for Jewish peddlers.

Sam Shubert was the first brother to work in a theater as a program boy and later as a ticket seller. At age 17, Sam produced his first play, a comedy about Washington politics. Within a year the Shubert brothers had leased theaters in Syracuse, Utica, Troy and Albany. They acquired their first theater in Manhattan (Broadway at Herald Square near the Metropolitan Opera House) in 1900.[18]

When Al Jolson left Dockstader's Minstrels (as the only Jew among 70 blackface minstrel men), he entered the vaudeville and musical comedy world controlled by immigrant Jews from Eastern Europe. And later when he went to Hollywood, the same ambitious immigrant Jews controlled the new film studios. Adolph Zukor from Hungary built Paramount Pictures. Louis B. Meyer from Russia headed Metro-Goldwyn-Mayer. William Fox from Hungary founded Fox Film Corporation. Harry, Sam, Albert and Jack Warner from Poland created Warner Brothers

For the first time in his life, Al Jolson was comfortable in his career with other Jewish East European immigrants. The show business moguls viewed from the outside world were 100 percent Americans. Among themselves they spoke an insider's jargon sprinkled with Yiddish, and fended off the hostility of many Christians who called Jews kikes and Christ killers.

In the period between the First and Second World Wars (the same time frame as the emergence of films as a major industry), anti-Semitism grew as a potent force in American life. Largely as a reaction to the two million East European Jews, most East coast colleges imposed quotas. Colgate allowed six Jews in the University in order to refute possible charges of anti-Semitism. In most colleges the quota hovered about three percent Jewish freshmen.[19]

While students were restricted, Jewish instructors were mostly banned. In 1927, the rule of tokenism prevailed at Yale, Princeton and the University of Chicago with one lone Jewish instructor. Columbia engaged two. Harvard had three. The City College of New York employed four.

The Jews who produced plays and films about American life created a masquerade (behind which they took cover). Al Jolson in his blackface disguise was the perfect front for the Shubert's Broadway musical shows. As Gus in the 1911 La Belle Paree, Jolson stood out because he was the only performer in blackface (Erastus Sparkler) and sang Paris Is A Paradise For Coons. The play had no story line but combined singers and dancers on a Cook's tour of Paris.

In each successive Broadway musical, 1911 Vera Violetta, 1912 The Whirl Of Society and 1913 The Honeymoon Express, Jolson plays a sassy blackface waiter or butler. The immigrant Jew as Broadway star (in productions controlled by immigrant Jews) works within a blackface minstrel tradition that obscures his Jewish pedigree, but proclaims his white identity. Jolson's slight Yiddish accent was hidden by a Southern veneer. In many interviews, the Jolson birthplace shifted from a obscure Russian village to the nation's capitol.

Yet, among themselves the core fact of life for Broadway and Hollywood Eastern European Jews was precisely their Jewishness. When Harry Warner first talked with Western Electric for a new sound system for motion pictures, he received exclusive rights for Warner Brothers studios. But Western Electric wanted to scuttle the agreement, and Warner threatened court action.

Then Harry Warner met with executives of Western Electric. He made an offer: "I will withdraw all our suits, if you'll do one thing. If you'll give me the name of one Jew who works for your company." Visibly embarrassed, the head of Western Electric research insisted that the company had no policy to exclude Jewish workers. He admitted that no Jewish employee could be named. Harry Warner gave his ultimatum, Warner does no business with companies that do not employ Jews. Within a week, Western Electric gave Warner Brothers exclusive sound rights.[20]

Al Jolson was the bridge between the silent films about Jewish life and the first talking movie where the story line is Jewish assimilation. For The Jazz Singer, a script and images evolved from

the silent films of the previous decade. The pioneer movie industry had filled the immense appetite of Jewish immigrants for stories about their life in America. In 1908 New York City had 123
movie theaters, 42 of which were on the Lower East Side.[21]

A dozen years before The Jazz Singer attempted to define the
meaning of life for Jews in America, Leo Frank, a Jew from New
York City was on trial for the murder of a white girl in Atlanta,
Georgia. Leo Frank's trial led to a newsreel-type documentary with
Frank's mother and Georgia Governor Slaton who commuted the
death sentence after disputed testimony.

For Jews in the United States, the trial in the South was the
reenactment of the European libel that Jews needed Christian blood
for their ritual sacrifices. Another film, The Frank Case, had a fictional trial in which the defendant was acquitted. The real case at
the time was on appeal before the Supreme Court. The appeal was
lost. Frank, who for his safety was placed on a prison farm, was
lynched in August 1915. A newsreel crew managed to capture
"the actual scenes of the lynching." The trial and lynching of Leo
Frank were among the earliest Jewish images on the silver screen.

Just two years before Jolson's Jazz Singer, a silent film with the
title His People dealt with the same conflicts—how Jewish can a
Jew be and still get ahead in America. Jolson, in real life and his
Jazz Singer film character, became Americanized by the artifice of
blackface. His Jewishness is irrelevant under the powerful status of
a white man. The characters in His People had no surefire remedy
for their Jewishness.

His People is a tale of a Jewish family's quest for an American
life-style in New York City during the 1920s. Two sons pursue
opposite interests: Sammy is a tough street fighter with his eye on
a boxing career and Morris is studious. Sammy also has his eye on
the Irish girl next door. Sammy, at last a man, fights under the
moniker, Battling Rooney. He wins his fight and loses his Jewishness
through a bogus Irish identity and an Irish sweetheart.

Morris is much more devious in his loss of Jewishness. He
meets the daughter of a retired (wealthy) judge and convinces her

that he's an orphan. He escapes the embarrassment of a stereotypical Jewish immigrant family and defines himself as a self-made man. He returns home to his parents when he needs money, claiming he cannot obtain a job unless he has a new suit. His father goes to a pawnshop in a blizzard, taking off his fur coat brought from Russia and trades it for a "new" suit for Morris. The suit is worthless to Morris who throws it into a trash can on the street.

The father develops pneumonia from the trek in the blizzard. Mother sends Morris a telegram to come home. Morris cannot explain to his fancy girlfriend that his father is dying and he must see him immediately. He had defined himself as an orphan. Father pulls through even without Morris, holding Sammy's hand believing in his delirium it is Morris'.

A few weeks later a neighbor recognizes Morris in the newspaper announcement of his upcoming wedding (an unfortunate orphan). Father goes to the bride's home where he encounters his son Morris. Rather than give up his orphan charade, Morris insists that he never set eyes on this man before. His father accepts the rejection and leaves quietly. But there is a happy ending when later Morris recants and father forgives all.[22]

His People enlists Jewish humor to portray the dilemma of many immigrants (and their American-born children) who wanted to discard their Jewishness. Samson Raphaelson's Jazz Singer side-stepped the Jewishness problem by evoking the symbol of blackface.

Exactly 80 years before the first talkie, Edwin P. Christy imposed a precise order on the minstrel show which was adopted by other troupes. By the time amateur groups took over the minstrel show, Christy's format was a ritual. The ritual transformed any differences among whites in the audience and on stage into a bond of social cohesion. Blackface, by mocking African Americans, brought native-born and immigrants under the umbrella of the white brotherhood.

Raphaelson did not have to reach deeply into his intellectual resources to understand the link between the traditional minstrel show and Jolson singing Mammy in blackface. The issue of Jewishness in America was resolved by a ritual which earlier helped Irish immigrants find their place in America.

Raphaelson saved the blackface performance for the end of his play, using aspects of Jolson's life as a youngster to dramatize one level of conflict for second generation Jews. At the surface level Jolson had to chose between a traditional way of life and the rewards of assimilation to an American life-style. The Jazz Singer appears to pit the American values of individualism and self-fulfillment against European values imposed by family and religious obligations.

The Jazz Singer has two dramatic scenes on the high holiday of Yom Kippur (the film caption uses the term Day of Atonement). At the start of the film, when Jackie Rabinowitz is 13 (the Jewish age for religious manhood), he manages to sing in a neighborhood saloon. A friend of his father who stops in for a frothy beer sees the boy and runs to the father's home next to the synagogue. Cantor Rabinowitz yanks Jackie out of the saloon. At home with mother Sara defending the boy, the Cantor takes Jackie into the bedroom for a strapping. Jackie warns the parents he will run away from home. As the Cantor and mother Sara go to the synagogue for Yom Kippur services, Jackie makes good on his promise.

About 10 years later (the film caption is vague on the passage of time), the audience sees Jackie working in a vaudeville theater in Chicago. Jolson the actor in 1927 was 40 years old (his hair thinning and his forehead graced by wrinkles), playing the part of a young man of 23 years. In Chicago Jackie receives a telegram, offering a top spot at the Winter Garden in New York City. This is his chance to visit his parents. At first the hugs and kisses between Jackie and mother Sara seem to point to reconciliation, even Cantor Rabinowitz smiles with happiness. But when the Cantor learns that Jackie will sing on Broadway, the bad mood returns. Jackie walks out again.

Time passes and Jackie has a Christian girlfriend, Mary Dale, who truly understands his conflict between family obligation and show business career. She encourages him to stick to his motto, "I live my life as I see fit."

On the big day of his Broadway opening as a star performer (which happens to be the evening of Yom Kippur), an elder from the synagogue comes to the theater. His father is very sick, perhaps on his death bed, and the Cantor's son, Jackie Rabinowitz, must sing in his place at the altar. Just as the elder appears in his room backstage, Jackie has finished applying his blackface makeup and covering his thinning hair with a black wooly wig.

This is the first time Jolson is seen in blackface. The audience knows this is the moment of truth. Yet, the truth is inexplicably interlaced with the symbolism of blackface. The scene has poetic poignancy, as the black mask represents the unique African American idiom of jazz and the death of old world culture. The scene is composed with exquisite seriousness.

Since The Jazz Singer is a Jewish film, Jackie redeems himself by canceling opening night, singing his father's role as cantor on Yom Kippur, and some time later at a special theater performance with his mother in the front row he sings Mammy on bended knee.

Hollywood Jews made The Jazz Singer, a film that asked the fundamental question: how can we assimilate in America and yet retain a Jewish identity? Loosely based on the career of Al Jolson, the film skirted the problem of Jewish identity. Jackie Rabinowitz— the representative for all show business Jews—resolved the conflict by courting a shiksa (a young non-Jewish woman), giving a token performance in the shul (synagogue), and pursuing all-out his blackface career on Broadway.

The covert message of The Jazz Singer is that the symbol of blackface provides the Jewish immigrant with the same rights and privileges accorded to earlier generations of European immigrants initiated into the rituals of the minstrel show.[23]

JOLSON THE SHLEMIEL

Even after The Jazz Singer, Jolson and the Jewish filmmakers examined the issues of turning Jews into Americans and the desire to have a Jewish identity (while disguised in a blackface mask). In each of eight Jolson films between 1927 and 1946, Jewishness and the blackface minstrel show define the themes. Jolson's life story (a different alias in each film) is the usual plot structure.

Less than a year after release of The Jazz Singer, Jolson starred in The Singing Fool. The 1928 film was yet another life of Al Jolson (with a sprinkle of blackface performer Eddie Cantor who started his career as a singing waiter). The film's title, Singing Fool, could in Yiddish become The Singing Shlemiel (which means a fool, a fall guy, a gullible person). Al plays a first-class shlemiel.[1]

The film opens in a New York City speakeasy where the singing waiter, Al Stone, expresses his ambition to write songs. He's trying to impress the blond shiksa singer, Molly Winton, who treats Al like dirt. But Al makes up his mind that if Molly hears the song he wrote just for her, she will open her heart to him.

A well-known theater producer, Mr. Marcus of the Loeb Theatre, and his white-tie buddy visit the speakeasy at the urging of two floozies. In order to gain entry, Mr. Marcus has to show his card to the doorman, who in turn informs the owner, Mr. Blackie. The Marcus party gets the best table in the house, and Al Stone is told about his "big chance."

Mr. Marcus is a fictional copy of Marcus Loew, the Jewish show business entrepreneur. Marcus Loew had started with one vaudeville theatre in 1903 and built a nationwide chain of movie houses. He then joined Louis B. Mayer in forming the M-G-M

Studio. Lowe had died one year before The Singing Fool premiered at the Winter Garden in New York City.

The actor, Edward Martindel, who played Loew was tall, distinguished, white-haired, with cultured speech (a gentleman of the old school). The real Loew (a hustler from the Lower East Side) lacked an imposing stature and handsome features. In the dream factory that was Hollywood the scene in the speakeasy was a memorial to a Jewish mogul of the film industry.[2]

Al Stone sings for Mr. Marcus who says there's a place in his Broadway show for a talented performer and creative songwriter. Molly, the blond shiksa, now cuddles up to Al and plants a juicy kiss on his lips. She and Al form a team for Mr. Marcus' show.

Time passes as Al Stone turns out one hit after another. Now Mrs. Molly Stone with Al's child, Sonny Boy, live in a luxury apartment. Al holds down two jobs (song writer and nightclub owner), so he asks his business manager, John Perry, to look after Molly because he's too busy.

One evening when Al comes home, he tries to snuggle up to Molly for a romantic encounter. She rebuffs him. Al goes into Sonny Boy's bedroom for affection from his child. Sonny Boy kisses daddy and raises his spirits. Al says to his son, "I don't know what I would do without you."

Sure enough, on New Year's Eve Molly and John run off together while Al is running a gala party at his nightclub. Molly leaves a note telling Al she's taking Sonny Boy because a child needs his mother. Al goes on the skids, stops shaving, stops working and hangs out on the streets.

His first employer, Mr. Blackie, takes Al into the speakeasy for a good meal. Al sees Grace, the cigarette girl, and realizes she truly loved him. Al and Grace start a new life.

Al receives word that Sonny Boy is in the hospital. He rushes to the bedside, takes up his child in his arms, and sings the theme song, Sonny Boy. Thinking he has revived the child, Al leaves the room. When he returns, the sheet is over the child's face.

That very night, Al must perform at the theater in blackface, singing Sonny Boy. He begs the stage manager to change the song, but the show must go on as scheduled. Al, singing out his heart, sees a vision of his son hovering above the audience. At the finale, Al collapses. The audience is wild with enthusiam for the emotional intensity of the performance.

In the parlance of Jewish show business, the final scenes of Sonny Boy were pure shmaltz. The Yiddish word captures that part of Jewish culture given to excessive sentimentality, pathos and mawkishness.

The Jewishness of The Singing Fool (Shlemiel) is evident in the New York City locale of the story and the show business plot. Jolson, in an unconscious parody of Jewish character, uses hand gestures more than words to communicate. He gushes emotions with his rolling eyes and distorted features.

When Jolson wore blackface only once in The Jazz Singer to sing Mammy, he honored his Jewish mother. In his second film, he wore blackface only once to lament Sonny Boy who did not have a Jewish mother. The hidden message for Jews was beware of blond shiksas.

Mammy, the 1930 film without plot or romance, treats the audience to a minstrel show, with intermissions for train travel, card games and visits with Al Fuller's (Jolson) mother. In the opening scene, Meadows Merry Minstrels and a brass band parade through the streets of a typical small town during a rain shower.[3]

The minstrels arrive at the theater, and once inside Al helps a fellow minstrel remove the wet high hat and satin top coat. Under the costume is Nora, the daughter of Mr. Meadows. Nora informs us why she must march with the boys, "since dad hasn't been able to pay salaries, he lost nearly all his men."

Al expresses concern about Nora's health because he loves her. He cannot tell her since she's engaged to his best friend, the tall, handsome interlocutor. Oddly, the interlocutor never kisses Nora or even holds her hand during the entire film. So much for the characters' love life.

That night 18 minstrels and nine musicians in formal attire and blackface makeup begin the show with a chorus of Here We Are. Mr. Bones (Al Fuller) then renders his solo: Who Paid the Rent for Mrs. Rip Van Winkle? The lyrics portray a woman whose husband disappears for 20 years and who has no visible means of support, yet keeps up the payments. Maybe the landlord (who departs with a smile on his face) was not expecting money, the song speculates.

Next a quartet harmonizes a sentimental favorite, When You and I Were Young Maggie. A patron in the minstrel audience runs his finger down the playbill to indicate to the movie audience that there was no shortage of musical routines. But the viewers were spared and the film moves to the finale. Six blackface minstrels come on stage in elaborate costumes (a female impersonator, a spanish outfit and a teutonic knight) and sing a mock opera—Yes We Have No Bananas.

The camera reminds the film-goer that the minstrel theater has more empty seats than paying customers. But one patron, who dresses and talks like an oaf, makes his way backstage. The oaf turns out to be a guardian angel who wants to join the troupe and has a farm worth $6,000 to bolster his dream. Lacking musical talent, the oaf becomes the new manager.

The film speeds along on the rails and the rejuvenated minstrel troupe has played in Philadelphia and Pittsburgh, bringing in $11,000. The new manager compares himself to a latter-day Barnum. At the request of Al Fuller, the train makes a brief stop in his hometown Cliffdale where his mother waits at the station.

Al's mother, with fair complexion and light eyes, displays a reserved manner yet conveying nuances of joy and sadness. The swarthy Jewish mother of The Jazz Singer wrings her hands and gushes tears. Jolson as Al Fuller is a midwestern small town WASP on the minstrel show circuit. Not a trace of Jewishness appears in the film Mammy.

At the next rail station the minstrels debark and parade through the streets of a much larger city. During the performance that

night, the large stage has 70 minstrels who execute in perfect unison
a tambourine chorus. The new manager/angel has restored the
company to its full compliment and upgraded the costumes and
stage settings that reflect an earlier era. Beginning in 1880
extravagant 100-man troupes were named Haverly's Mastodons,
Leavitt's Gigantean Minstrels and Hooley's Megatherians.

The mega-minstrel troupes provided spectacular street parades.
One minstrel company had 110 members, two bands of 14 musicians each, a sextette of saxophone players, two drum corps of eight
each, two drum majors and a quartette of mounted buglers. The
street parade evolved as a ceremonial ritual augmenting and expanding the blackface stage ritual to the world outside of the theater. The minstrels emulated the premiere American secular ritual:
the Fourth of July parade.[4]

The film Mammy starts with a small town street parade of the
minstrels slushing in the rain and ends with an invigorated troupe
marching through the streets of a big city. Along the city's parade
route there appears among the white crowds a genuine black woman
in Aunt Jemima costume who Al Fuller gleefully acknowledges as
"Mammy." The film's title finds its meaning in the final symbolic
image.

Mammy is the third film in the Hollywood minstrel cycle
that began with the Jazz Singer of 1927. Al Fuller (Jolson) has no
trace of Jewishness. His bloodline (through the fair white mother)
is Nordic. But Jolson's real-life stage history is accurate in the film.
The manager of the revived Meadows troupe looks like Lew Dockstader
for whom Jolson worked during the 1908-1909 season.

By intention or not, the film Mammy makes a statement about
the revival of the minstrel show in American popular culture. When
the professional minstrel venue moved from the stage to the screen,
a vast new audience embraced the ceremonial rituals of blackface.

For his other 1930 film, Big Boy, Jolson departs from the formula of a white entertainer who sings in blackface. Big Boy is a
race horse and Jolson is Gus the jockey who wins the Kentucky
Derby in spite of mobsters who connive to fix the race. Jolson

appears in blackface from beginning to end. When the film audience thinks the story is over, Jolson (in suit and tie) and the cast appear on a stage. The film is transformed into a stage play where the actors line up for bows. Was this a ploy to make sure everyone in the movie audience sees Jolson's true white identity? Standing on the stage, Jolson thanks the cast for their performances and the cast in return asks Jolson to sing a song.[5]

Before singing, Jolson tells a story about his Grandfather Moshe and describes looking for his home and seeing a ham hanging in the window and knowing that was not his home. His story of Jewishness has an untruth. As an Eastern European immigrant, Jolson wants to distance himself from his first generation status. Grandfather Moshe is in reality his father, Cantor Moshe Yoelson. The curtain call sends the message that under the blackface I may be Jewish, but I am definitely white.

In the 1934 film, Wonder Bar, Jolson uses blackface parody to create the most offensive travesty in a Hollywood film. As Al Wonder, Jolson is a suave American who owns the Wonder Bar, a high-class cabaret in Paris. The clients of Wonder Bar include down-on-their-luck royalty, rich middle-aged American couples, and an assortment of gigolos and fancy-dressed women who cater to the whims of middle-aged men and women looking for a new thrill. Each of the musical and dance numbers within the cabaret has a European or exotic Latin flavor (Dolores Del Rio and Ricardo Cortez provide the dance action).[6]

Then at the climax of the cabaret's entertainment Jolson (Al Wonder) comes on stage in blackface leading a mule. The stage is magically transformed into a vast landscape with a rainbow as a road to some distant place in the sky. The audience understands that his time on earth is at an end. He mounts the mule and follows the rainbow road. Jolson knocks on heaven's door.

He and the mule enter under the escort of two blackface angels who guide him to St. Peter, a large blackface man with white whiskers, dressed in a white gown with angel's wings attached at his shoulders. Jolson, hanging on to the mule's bridle, is next introduced to Gabriel, another white-haired gentleman in blackface wearing a white gown and angel's wings.

Three small children in blackface, white gowns and angel's wings accompany Jolson and St. Peter to Pork Chop Orchard and Possum Pie Grove, identified by a large sign. Jolson, pulling a pork chop from a tree in the orchard, notices Old Black Joe strumming on his banjo. As Jolson walks with St. Peter he encounters Uncle Tom.

On the heavenly path Jolson and St. Peter meet the blackface angel in a chef's cap who runs a chicken rotisserie where live chickens are selected, feathers plucked and the birds turned on a spit until perfectly done. In no time at all, half a chicken shows up on a plate with the fixings.

Jolson is distracted from eating the succulent chicken leg when St. Peter invites him to board a trolly that travels from the "Milky Way to Lenox." As the trolly enters Harlem, Jolson sees dozens of blackface winged angels in white gowns strutting in the streets. A stand piled high with watermelons has a sign: "Take One."

Next Jolson and St. Peter arrive at the door to a barbershop. The sign states: "Shine 10¢, Shave 25¢, Wings Trimmed 35¢." Jolson sits in a barber chair then looks at the men in top hats and white gowns on either side of him with newspapers. He stands up and whistles to an angel who flies to him with a newspaper. Jolson opens the paper so that the front page faces the camera, and in the close-up fills the screen.

The audience sees that the front page, written in Hebrew characters, is a Yiddish newspaper. Those in the audience who can read Yiddish can identify the paper as "The Garden of Eden Star." The headline translates as "Angels Greet with Open Hands." Jolson's face pops up above the Yiddish newspaper and he nods in approval. While many American Jews and others in the audience could not read Yiddish (the newspaper had a hidden message for some Jews), most in the movie audience recognized the paper as Yiddish or Jewish. It was Jolson's intention to convey that behind the blackface mask was a Jew.

Jolson and St. Peter leave the barbershop and follow a street parade with a brass band for a minstrel performance of "Uncle Tom." They drop out of the street parade at the entrance to the "Big Dipper Cabaret." Within the vast heavenly cabaret is a stage with a performance in progress with dozens of chorus girls (white girls wearing blackface makeup and black hose).

The stage is surrounded by hundreds of tables, but at one St. Peter and Jolson sit down with the Emperor Jones (the lead character from a play by Eugene O'Neill). Jolson finds a pair of dice on the table and proceeds to win from the Emperor all the medals pinned on his chest and the military ornaments on his white gown, so that Jolson ends up with the decorations on his gown.

During the crap game, the stage show features a blackface tap dancer who emerges from a eight-foot high watermelon, neatly cut into slices carried by the chorus girls. The male tap dancer wears a short white gown, black hose, white spats on his shoes, and a silver top hat (of course, he has a pair of wings).

After the tap dance, the camera pulls back so the movie audience can see the cabaret audience cheering the stage show. St. Peter beckons Jolson to follow him to an immense open cloud garden where about 200 blackface angels on their knees sway their arms above their heads in rhythm to the theme song, Goin' To Heaven On A Mule. The musical number ends with Jolson and St. Peter in the middle of the chorus of blackface angels raising their arms in final praise.

In the entire history of blackface performance from Edwin P. Christy (with less than a dozen men) to Lew Dockstader's Minstrels (with 70 men), Goin' To Heaven On A Mule is the largest minstrel show ever mounted with 200 men and women. With worldwide distribution, Al Jolson's blackface heaven was seen by tens of millions in the United States, Europe and South America.

Goin' To Heaven On A Mule was a minstrel show parody of a serious play. The play, Green Pastures by Marc Connelly, was first produced at the Mansfield Theatre in New York City in 1930. Green Pastures, won a Pulitzer Prize for Connelly, a white journalist.

Theater critics proclaimed Green Pastures a "classic," and Bennett Cerf wrote the "play has become a genuine part of American dramatic culture." Today most white critics and black critics would see the Green Pasture characters as stereotypes. But in 1930 Marc Connelly was a rare white man who wrote sympathic stage portraits of African Americans.[7]

Green Pastures is a fable comparing 1928 with biblical times. In a black church in Louisiana an old preacher teaches a group of boys and girls in a Sunday School. The preacher tells the children that before God made the earth, there was nothing but angels. As the play progresses, scenes from the bible—Adam and Eve, Noah, Isaac and Jacob, Moses, Pharaoh—come to life before the eyes of the children.

It was Connelly's intention by replacing Hebrews with American blacks in the Old Testament to show their strengths as a result of suffering, and envision a religious and social redemption. Green Pastures had black actors (not whites in blackface which was common in plays and musicals of the 1920s).

Jolson's Goin' To Heaven On A Mule production within the film, Wonder Bar, was a mockery of black religous practices interwoven with the minstrel tradition of watermelon and chicken eating, dice playing and 24-hour dance and song reveling.

For Wonder Bar, Jolson was the Jewish owner of a night club in Paris (with a compulsion to perform in blackface extravaganzas). His Jewishness is not an overt description of the character, Al Wonder. But the most obvious clue is in the name, Al (who can be no other than Al Jolson) the same Al who made earlier films to display his blackface singing style.

Jolson, as Al Howard, plays a stage and nightclub performer in the 1935 Go Into Your Dance. His first blackface number, About A Quarter to Nine, takes place within the film at Chicago's elegant St. Ledger Roof. With a chorus of about 32 men dressed in white tie and cutaway, Jolson sings and dances.[8]

The male chorus follows Jolson across the stage to a platform setting where Jolson changes the song to Swanee, and in an instant at the sound of the magic words the chorus turns into a minstrel troupe in cutaway coats, and the black top hats are now silver top hats to contrast with the blackface makeup. Jolson and the male chorus spend a minute in the past, as the men tap their tambourines in rhythm to the music. In a wink of the eye the chorus is once again white faces with black top hats and no tambourines.

Jolson (Al Howard) returns to his dressing room. When he sees his male servant in the room, Jolson says: Snowflake, go to the graveyard and get your lunch. Snowflake replies: Don't talk about graveyards Mr. Howard 'cause I even get scared with the lights on. Snowflake is a rather dark African American with obvious devotion to his boss. He is a little slow mentally and gets confused about how white show business works. But Al Howard is so fond of Snowflake that he knocks on his head for good luck.

Al Howard moves to New York City (The Greatest Jewish City in the World) where he remodels a theatre into a cabaret by the name of Casino de Paree. Jolson sings the final song, Go Into Your Dance, in blackface. Like the other Al characters in his earlier films, Jolson is gushy when expressing his feelings (with excessive hand gestures).

By 1936, the scenario for a Jolson film cannibalized title, songs and plots from each of the previous Hollywood ventures. The 1936 title (The Singing Kid) reminds everyone of 1928 (The Singing Fool).[9]

The 1936 film (The Singing Kid) starts with a medley of Jolson songs: Mammy; Swanee; Rock-a-Bye Your Baby; California, Here I Come; April Showers; About a Quarter to Nine; and Sonny Boy. In blackface for all but two, Jolson reproduces the first part of a minstrel show.

Somewhere in the middle of the film, Jolson appears in a minstrel show part two when he leads a large chorus of black singers and dancers in a musical extravaganza. Jolson in blackface has about 100 members of a chorus back him up as he sings, Save Me Sister. What appears to be a gospel number turns into a jazzy love song. Jolson and the chorus ascend a flight of stairs into clouds. The film transends itself into a black heaven with genuine African Americans instead of the blackface angels in the 1934 Wonder Bar. Hollywood intentionally confuses the social message of the minstrel show.

Near the end of the film, a third minstrel act takes place in the streets of New York City (in the traditional minstrel show, the finale could be a plantation scene). Jolson and a male quartet roam the city streets, enlisting the pedestrians to join in the fun. Only Jolson and the quartet get to wear blackface. Once in The Singing Kid film he tells a sidekick "You're a shlemiel."

In between the three minstrel parts, the film alludes to Jolson's stage and radio career. Between April of 1935 and March of 1936, Jolson made 39 broadcasts for the NBC network on Saturday nights.[10]

When Al Jolson was 60 years old, Columbia Pictures produced The Jolson Story with Larry Parks as Al Jolson and the real singing voice of Jolson. Most screen biographies come after the death of the famous person. Jolson was the only celebrity to have two movies about his life and to have roles in both productions. When he was 41 Jolson starred in The Jazz Singer based on a Broadway play in which his life story matches that of the main character (but with a different name).[11]

The same theme which dominated The Jazz Singer of 1927 also dictated how the 1946 film biography unfolded. For an Eastern European Jewish immigrant to achieve the American dream, he must obscure the outward signs of his Jewishness. The Jolson Story begins with young Asa Yoelson (Al Jolson) in the balcony of Kernan's Burlesque Theatre in Washington, D.C., as Steve Martin performs on the stage. Part clown, part comic and mostly violinist and cellist, Martin invites the audience to sing along when he plays Banks of the Wabash.

Asa is the only one to sing. Martin is impressed with his voice as well as his daring, and asks him for his name. When asked where he learned to sing like that, Asa replies the synagogue. Asa leaves the theater in a hurry as he is late for services at the synagogue. Asa joins the synagogue choir in his prayer shaw and yarmulka (skull-cap). Later at home Asa is questioned by his father, Cantor Yoelson, about his tardiness. Before Asa can explain, Steve Martin shows up at the cantor's door.

Martin tells Cantor and mother Yoelson (in reality at that time his mother had died and the cantor's wife was Asa's step-mother) that Asa has a future in show business. He offers Asa a spot in his act, starting the next day in Baltimore.

Cantor Yoelson refuses and Martin leaves. Asa must promise never to go a theater again. He says he can't promise. That night Asa runs away from home, hopping a freight train to find Steve Martin in Baltimore. Asa, picked up by police, is taken to St. Mary's Home for Boys where he explains that he has a job singing for Steve Martin. The priest, inspired by Asa's claim, places him in the choir.

In the next scene Asa in the choir renders Ave Maria with great feeling. Meanwhile Steve Martin and the Yoelsons arrive at the Boys Home. The priest leads them into the chapel to see and hear Asa. Cantor Yoelson says "singing without his cap on." The priest retorts "it's not what's on your head, but in your heart." Cantor Yoelson, put down by the priest, says nothing but displays a sheep-ish grin.

The issue of wearing a yarmulka is repeated a number of times in the film as the quintessential sign of Jewishness. Orthodox Jews, such as Cantor Yoelson, wear a yarmulka at home and at work, as well as in the synagogue. Even non-religious Jewish males will wear a yarmulka at a funeral, a wedding or a Bar Mitzvah. The yarmulka is a sign of respect before God.

In the film, young Asa must wear a yarmulka when he runs from the theater into the synagogue. The next time a yarmulka figures as a potent symbol is when Al now a man returns home from a road tour. He sits down to a meal with his parents, and as mother Yoelson places his plate on the table she discretely slips Al a yarmulka. She stands between the Cantor and Al so he can quickly put it on his head. Spying the cap, the Cantor asks, "did you wear

one all the time you were away?" Al admits, "as a matter of fact I
didn't." Cantor Yoelson (who is wearing his cap) relents, "for me
it's not neccessary."

Much later in the film, Cantor and mother Yoelson are brought
to California in celebration of their wedding anniversary. While
staying in their son's new home, the couple have two meals. The
first meal in the early afternoon is an outdoor luncheon where the
film audience may be surprised to see the Cantor eating without
his yarmulka. Then in the evening at a formal dinner, the Cantor
again appears with no yarmulka. No character at either meal says
"Cantor where's your cap?" Since the yarmulka played so key a
role in previous scenes, the missing cap at the California meals was
a subliminal, yet powerful, message about assimilation.

At the St. Mary's Home for Boys in Baltimore early in the film
the priest, who sends for the Yoelsons and Steve Martin to identify
young Asa, negotiates a new life for the boy. Vouching for the
good reputation of Martin, the priest convinces the Yoelsons that
Asa should take to the road as a performer. Steve Martin became
father, mother and mentor. For Jolson's crucial years of adoles-
cence, Steve Martin was his only family.

Young Asa kept in touch with his folks in Washington by picture post cards from the cities on the vaudeville tour. The Yoelsons
set aside a wall for the post cards, and with pride (mixed with
sadness) they read the names—Philadelphia, Pittsburgh and Indianapolis. Cantor Yoelson verbally stumbled when he read
"Dubuque, Iowa." The word became "Dybbuk." Did the insider's
Yiddish expression refer to young Asa's wandering across America
or did it touch on a more somber image?

In Eastern European Jewish folklore Dybbuk is the wandering
soul of the dead. When production of The Jolson Story began in
1945, the death camps were a new concept for the Jews in America.
Only one year earlier the first reports about Auschwitz appeared
in American newspapers. A Swiss refugee organization issued a
document that included interviews with a few Jews who had escaped
from Auschwitz. The eyewitness testimony about the operation of

the extermination camps for Jews included the tattooing of numbers on the skin of victims (as a method of keeping count). One excapee had a "six-numeral figure above the 200,000 mark on his leg." The Rev. Paul Vogt, who headed the Swiss investigation, estimated that 1,715,000 Jews were murdered at Auschwitz as of April 15, 1944.[12]

As Asa and Steve Martin travel from city to city on the train, Jolson receives his schooling. In one short scene, Martin tests Asa's spelling with the word, tedious. Approaching manhood, Asa is photographed in his first pair of long pants for his folks in Washington. Then Martin promotes Jolson, rewarding him with his name on the bill. At that moment, Martin decides Asa Yoelson lacks the American sound, and "baptizes" him as Al Jolson.

In Lousville, Kentucky during the Derby, minstrel impresario Lew Dockstader visits the theater where Martin and Jolson perform. By accident, Jolson discovers that blackface singer Tom Baron is on his back in a drunken stupor. He seizes the chance to be a soloist by disguising himself in blackface makeup and wearing Baron's stage outfit. After Jolson's masquerade as Tom Baron, Dockstader goes backstage (sees black makeup behind Jolson's ear) and makes a handsome offer to the right man. The film is purely fictional in tracing Jolson's career, but has a hidden truth about Jews in Hollywood.

Jolson profusely rejects his opportunity of a lifetime on the grounds that he cannot leave his surrogate father, Steve Martin. When in Baltimore at the Boys' Home, Jolson eagerly abandoned his Jewish father. Martin convinces his young ward that his future in show business depends on his decision now. Jolson, with agonizing guilt, joins up with Dockstader's minstrels.

In a short time, Jolson is disillusioned with his role in a quartet. He complains to Dockstader and now has a role in a singing duet. Still not satisfied, he misses a performance in New Orleans while seeking out black jazz. When he returns to the theater, Dockstader tells Al "to call it quits." Al says, "I think you're right."

The true story of Jolson and Dockstader was different. Al Jolson had third billing under Lew Dockstader and Neil O'Brien (a seasoned blackface performer). Jolson ran out on Dockstader to star in another minstrel show, but he had to return because of a contract. With the help of the Schubert brothers, the contract was voided by Dockstader.

Luck and coincidence in the film version of Jolson's career land him in the show at New York City's Winter Garden Theatre. He rapidly rises in the cast from underling to star. A chance meeting with dancer Julie Benson opens Al's eyes to romance. The couple clicks, work keeps them apart, love conquers all, and the pair elopes to Connecticut. The film's Julie Benson represents Ruby Keeler (his third wife from 1928 to 1939).

Immediately after the wedding, the couple visit Al's parents in Washington. As soon as they walk in the door, dinner is served—beware of the horseradish, the new husband warns too late. (Cantor Yoelson has a cap on his head in this scene.) Dinners seem to dominate the motion picture when Jolson is not singing. Gentiles celebrate by drinking, but Jews celebrate by eating—says comic Jackie Mason.

The last dinner in the film takes place in Jolson's California home for the celebration of the wedding anniversary of the Yoelsons. In the marriage between Jolson and Julie Benson the ceremony is off camera by a judge with no relatives present. In contrast, the Yoelsons magically recreate their wedding as they dance to Jolson's emotional rendering of the Anniversary Song. The movie's message for the audience is that Jewish culture as an integral part of life experience exists only as memory in the lives of the immigrant parents.

The Jazz Singer of 1927 defined an era of Jewish immigrant life in America in which the past must be cast off. Virtually all of Jewish culture had to be abandoned. The Jew in blackface had the perfect disguise to proclaim his new identity as a white citizen of a white nation. Jolson's motion pictures during the 1930s made no overt reference to Jewishness. Hollywood had taken its own advice after 1927 to merge Jewish identity with the white majority. For the next 20 years Jewish images disappeared from the silver screen, leaving only the blackface minstrel show in Hollywood as a reference point to who was truly white.

The Jolson Story of 1946 re-evaluated Jewish culture by the comparison of Mr. and Mrs. Jolson with Cantor and Mrs. Yoelson. The film tells of the success of American Jews in their careers. They traded Jewish culture and Jewish family life for American success. Was the Dybbuk in The Jolson Story a recognition of Jewish souls from Europe wandering in the consciousness of American Jews?

By 1950 when George Jessel delivered his eulogy for Al Jolson, the Jews in the United States knew the Jewish death toll in Europe was six million. The 1,000-year-old Jewish civilization centered in Poland and Lithuania (Jolson's native land) was annihilated. Jessel said Jolson "told the world that the Jew in America did not have to sing in sorrow, but could shout happily about Dixie."[13]

Jessel made a distinction between Jews in the United States and the rest of the world (which really meant Europe). Singing happily about Dixie for the 90 percent of Jews who lived in the big cities of the North was a metaphor for the Jewish status as white citizens in a country where legal segregation and social custom made blacks the aliens of the land.

"When he (Jolson) cried Mammy, it was in appreciation, not in lament." Jessel's use of the word, "lament," evokes the Jewish prayer for the dead which in his heart he knew were the Jews of Europe. Mammy is a black Mammy who shielded American Jews from fatally violent anti-Semitism, and for that he was truly appreciative.

George Jessel was the original Jazz Singer. He starred in Samson Raphaelson's stage play, giving over one thousand performances. When Jessel was offered the same role in the film version (the historic transformation of motion pictures), he wanted an extra $10,000 to cover any risks to his career. The Warner brothers beckoned to Jolson who was eager to take part in the sound experiment. Jessel confessed afterwards that he made the mistake of his life.[14]

Jessel was a professional sidekick of Eddie Cantor (the only other blackface entertainer to rival Jolson). Cantor and Jessel had featured parts in the 1912 Kid Kabaret, a vaudeville troupe on the Orpheum circuit (the number one booking that included the Palace Theatre in Manhattan). Cantor played a blackface butler for a rich couple who went out for an evening of fun and left their son at home in Cantor's care. The son invited his friends to stage their own cabaret under the butler's direction.[15]

Cantor, the eldest in the troupe, was 20 and Jessel was 14. Jessel had the role of Muttky, described in the program as "a little bit of Yiddish." Cantor's blackface butler impersonated Al Jolson, and to his surprise during a booking in Oakland, California, Jolson showed up backstage. Both Jessel and Cantor received warm compliments from Jolson. Cantor first saw Jolson perform in vaudeville at Hammerstein's in New York City. In an interview years later, Cantor said, "He (Jolson) was my idol. There was something electric about him that sent a thrill up your spine."

The success of blackface Al Jolson at Warner Brothers gave producer Samuel Goldwyn the inspiration to lure Eddie Cantor away from Broadway. As a Jewish immigrant (Schmuel Gelbfisz) from Poland, Goldwyn rose from glove salesman to film studio executive. He was the Goldwyn in Metro-Goldwyn-Mayer (M-G-M), but in name only. Others controlled the company. Eddie Cantor (the son of Jewish immigrants) was born on the Lower East Side of Manahhtan. His name was Isidore Iskowitz. Both his mother and father died before he turned three, and Grandma Esther Kantrowitz at age 62 became his only parent.[16]

As a youngster, Cantor entered many amateur contests at local theaters, usually in blackface. Finding his niche in vaudeville, Cantor perfected his blackface persona. For his first role in a Samuel Goldwyn musical film (Whoopee), Cantor played the part of a New York City hypochondriac who had attended Hebrew School. Cantor was the quintessential nebbish—the Yiddish word for a

timid and fearful man. Decades later, Woody Allen cultivated the
nebbish persona to perfection.[17]

Goldwyn found the ideal Western ranch where a New York
City hypochondriac could recover from his imagined illnesses.
Cantor's greatest struggle in the film, however, was defending himself from the sexual advances of his nurse. By accident, Cantor
finds himself covered in blackface makeup (he hid in an oven that
caught fire). He takes the opportunity to sing a minstrel-like tune.

In another Goldwyn musical (Roman Scandals), Cantor and
the cast are magically transported to ancient Rome. Again, by accident, Cantor is covered in a facial mud mask (with a group of
women in a public bath). He passes himself off as an Ethiopian
beauty expert who sings "Keep Young and Beautiful."[18]

In Goldwyn's Kid Millions, Cantor is a Brooklyn waif who
inherits 77 million from a father he never saw. In order to collect
the fortune, Cantor must travel to Egypt. Ethel Merman (who
knew his father) follows Cantor on the ship to Egypt and claims
she's his mother while attempting to seduce him in his cabin.[19]

Once out to sea, Cantor and Merman enlist the crew and pas-
sengers in an old fashioned minstrel show. Cantor wears sparkling
white formal tails and top hat to contrast with his black makeup.
The show's tunes include I Want to Be a Minstrel Man and Irving
Berlin's Mandy.

Samuel Goldwyn produced six films for Eddie Cantor between
1930 and 1935, all box office successes. Yet, like Eddie Cantor
himself the films loss their sparkle. The Hollywood minstrel show
had gone out of fashion. Then M-G-M paired Mickey Rooney
and Judy Garland in two musical films that revived the minstrel
tradition.

In 1939 Judy Garland and Mickey Rooney (voted the world's
most popular performer) starred in Babes in Arms. Rooney
displayed his charisma by organizing talented teenagers in an
amateur minstrel show. Using a farm barn as the stage, Garland
introduces the show (singing in whiteface) with My Daddy Was A
Minstrel Man (I'd like to black my face).[20]

Before she can finish her song, a parade of blackface young-sters with a brass band march down the center aisle towards the stage. They carry banners that read "Dixie Minstrels" while sing-ing Stephen Foster's Camptown Races. The camera moves back-stage where Rooney and Garland are covering their faces in black makeup. It was a convention in blackface scenes to have the film audience see the white actors applying black makeup (leaving no doubt that minstrels really were white).

Some 24 minstrels in satin cutaways and top hats sing and dance to Foster's Oh! Susanna. Then the interlocutor (the tallest man on the stage), dressed in white tie and tails and face free of black makeup, instructs the assembly, "Gentlemen, be seated."

Next the elegant interlocutor introduces the endmen, Mr. Bones (Mickey Rooney) and Mr. Tambo (Judy Garland). Both are fitted in identical costumes of striped hat, white shirt, plaid vest, white stockings and dark pants that reach mid-calf (reminiscent of a clown costume).

Following the old tradition, the interlocutor says to Mr. Bones, "I have a question to ask—who was that lady I saw you with last night?" Mr. Bones explodes in laughter before answering with "that was no lady that was my wife."

One departure from tradition is the real female (Garland) rather than the female impersonator which was integral to minstrel show parody. Seven minutes into the amateur minstrel show (a chorus of the sentimental Moonlight Bay and a solo by Judy Garland) a sudden rain storm drives away the audience seated in the open in front of the barn.

M-G-M two years later produced a second minstrel show, grander in scale and clearly the high point of the film. The same stars (Garland and Rooney), the same plot (stage-struck young-sters seeking fame), and nearly the same title (1939 Babes in Arms, 1941 Babes on Broadway) meant the minstrel show had currency.[21]

The 1941 Babes on Broadway provided 12 minutes of a min-strel show as the grand finale with 64 minstrels (up from 24), and using a professional theater rather than a barn. Garland and Rooney, again in the roles of Mr. Tambo and Mr. Bones, wear the same costumes of plaid vests, striped hats and shortened pants. Were the costumes retrieved from the wardrobe storage of the 1939 film in order to preserve a tradition?

A group of young performers on an empty stage decide to produce a good old fashioned minstrel show and immediately sing the theme for the show (Blackout over Broadway). The camera backstage catches Rooney and Garland applying blackface makeup in front of a mirror. Before they finish (with their faces only half black), Rooney and Garland pass black makeup, using a tambourine as a tray, to the young cast members.

The curtain goes up and the 64 minstrels sing and dance to the tune of Blackout over Broadway. Dressed in white tie and tails, the interlocutor announces, "Gentlemen, be seated." He then walks to stage left where Mr. Tambo (Judy Garland) sits at the end of a row of minstrels. The intrlocutor asks, "Mr. Tambo, Mr. Tambo how do you do, and incidentally, how do you feel?"

Mr. Tambo, seated with one leg thrown up on the armrest (a vulgar fellow when compared with the perfect decorum of the minstrels who sit with their knees nearly touching), arises and struts across the stage to the interlocutor. "I feel like a stove pipe." The interlocutor repeats, "you feel like a stove pipe." Tambo says, "Yeah, sooty," and laughs at his own witticism.

The interlocutor reminds the audience that minstrels love to dance as he introduces Rufus Rastus Jefferson Davis Brown, a blackface tap dancer dressed immaculately in white. Next, Tambo is called upon to sing, and he (Garland) belts out a new song, Franklin D. Roosevelt Jones, which exorts the virtues of naming a black baby for the president.

Mr. Bones (Rooney) performs a virtuoso solo (Old Folks at Home) on the banjo, followed by 12-piece banjo band strumming Alabamy Bound. In between the performances, the camera focuses on the audience, showing one couple expressing unconditional delight with the minstrels. At last the show comes to an end with the minstrels singing and tap dancing to Waiting for The Robert E. Lee (introduced by Al Jolson in The Jazz Singer).

When M-G-M produced Babes in Arms in 1939, war jitters infected Europe. The film's major musical number besides the minstrel show was God's Country which alluded to the fuhrer and the goosestep across the ocean (America doesn't have to worry).

By 1941, with battles in Asia and Europe and the United States committed to the European Allies, American participation in World War II was a certainty. Yet, no hint of worldwide conflict emerged from the 1941 Babes on Broadway.

The minstrel show—from the Civil War, the Spanish American War, and World War I to the Second World War—was a secular ritual that provided social cohesion for whites (be they native born or immigrants from Europe) by mocking African Americans as peculiar outsiders.

Anthropologists use a set of markers to identify secular rituals in any region of the world.[22]

(1) Repetition of form (format). Since 1847 when Edwin P. Christy introduced the Interlocutor, Mr. Tambo and Mr. Bones, the minstrel show has not wavered from his conception of characters and their roles. The interlocutor asks straight-faced questions and the endmen reply with comic exaggeration. Christy designed their costumes which balanced the highly formal attire of the minstrels with the mismatched vestments of the clown-like endmen. Christy formulated the three parts of the show: the walk-on with introductions of the endmen by the interlocutor, questions by the interlocutor, song and instrumental solos; the second part or olio could be anything— trained dog, magic, singing, dancing or banjo duets; the third part consisted of a parody of an opera or an elaborate re-enactment of joyful plantation life.

(2) "Special" behavior or symbols. The ubiquitous use of blackface makeup was the core symbol of the minstrel show combined with parody of black culture.

(3) Order—an organized event, having a beginning and an end. Order is the dominant mode and is often quite exaggeratedly precise. Christy's three parts and the strict control of part one by the interlocutor distinguishes the minstrel show from any other "entertainment."

(4) By definition ritual has a social meaning. Its very occurance contains a social message. The minstrel show ritual symbolizes the social cohesion of the assembled group and simultaneously acts as the vehicle for bringing about social solidarity for the white cast on stage and and white people seated in the audience.

The minstrel show endured with the same essential format from Christy's 1847 minstrel hall to the 1941 M-G-M Babes on Broadway. What started as an entertainment for New Yorkers (many of whom recent immigrants from Ireland) evolved into a ritual of social inclusion, social cohesion and social solidarity for whites.

The Warner brothers and Al Jolson recognized the ambivalent status of immigrant Jews (their own status) in America during the 1920s and 1930s. The minstrel show, as transformed by Edwin P. Christy into a secular ritual, provided Hollywood Jews a white identity (in blackface).

When M-G-M produced Babes on Broadway in 1941 with its blackface grand finale, the United States had taken sides in the struggle between England and Germany. America joined ideologically with the good guys. The minstrel show, in its own way, was a rallying point for a 100-year heritage of white men's unity.

STRUTTING TO REDEMPTION

For white audiences the blackface minstrel show was a platform for the ridicule of blacks, serving to reinforce cohesion among whites. At the end of the Civil War a new type of minstrel show emerged from the South, controlled by white managers who recruited ex-slaves for all-colored minstrel troupes. Among the first to tour the Northern cities were Brooker and Clayton's Georgia Minstrels ("The Only Simon Pure Negro Troupe in the World").

The colored minstrels were a mirror image of the blackface (white) shows, including black makeup and painted grotesque lips. No colored troupe performing for white audiences in the North survived for long. During Dan Bryant's reign from 1857 to 1875, only two colored troupes appeared in New York City. The Georgia Minstrels, "a band of real colored folk," were at 600 Broadway on September 9, 1868. Five years later, Callender's Georgia Minstrels performed in Hooley's Opera House in Brooklyn on August 10, 1873.[1]

In the South, however, colored minstrel shows had enthusiastic African American audiences. Colored troupes performed for black audiences in small towns and major cities. In 1869 Hicks and Heights Georgia Minstrels had an enthusiastic reception by the African American community of Washington, D.C. The most enduring troupe, Rabbit Foot Minstrels, performed for black audiences in the South. The company, founded in 1900 in Port Gibson, Mississippi, was the top show for black audiences for decades.

As white minstrel shows faded into vaudeville, the colored shows also evolved. Blues singers "Ma" Rainey and Bessie Smith polished their style with the Rabbit Foot Minstrels.[2]

Ernest Hogan, who learned his stage craft in colored minstrel shows, was the pivotal performer who began the transformation of the stage of ridicule to an authentic display of black culture. Hogan wrote songs (the most famous of the era, All Coons Look Alike To Me), managed his own minstrel troupe that played in Australia and Hawaii, as well as starring as actor, comedian and dancer in black shows for white audiences on Broadway. The 1898 New York City production of Clorindy; or, the Origin of The Cakewalk made Hogan the highest paid black performer.

Ernest Hogan, born in 1865 in Bowling Green, Kentucky, belonged to a new generation of blacks in the South. Under slavery black children were trained by their parents to humble themselves when in the presence of whites. A slave displaying pride by erect posture and a spring in his step could feel the lash for infringing the etiquette of subservience. Hogan, as a child, had no barriers to free expression of his personality and talent.

Hogan began his career as a "pickaninny" in a touring company of Uncle Tom's Cabin. He graduated to tent shows that featured black performers in the sideshows of a circus. Many traveling medicine shows also depended on black tent shows to entice spectators. The pitch for the cure-all elixir came along with the excitement of black song and dance.

Sometime during his youthful tours with tent shows, he changed his birthname (Reuben Crowdus) to an Irish name. The Irish for years were the most popular blackface minstrels. After his apprenticeship with tent shows, Hogan joined the colored Pringle's Georgia Minstrels. He learned the formula devised by Edwin P. Christy three decades earlier. The colored minstrels used the same formula of three parts, the same songs and black makeup. A troupe could only be a minstrel show if black makeup covered the face of whites or blacks.

Under the banner of Eaton and Hogan's Colored Minstrels, Hogan appeared in Chicago December 9, 1891. The group went on to San Francisco. There's no record of Hogan's stage performances for several years until he published a song in 1895. With words and music by Hogan, the song became one of the most popular in the country. His All Coons Look Alike To Me inspired a ten-year flood of "coon" songs from Tin Pan Alley. White composers dominated the new "coon" song fad, and gave voice to the racial attitudes of the time.[3]

Hogan, trained in the minstrel tradition, evoked the stereotypes of black romance in his song.

> Talk about a coon having trouble, think I have
> enough of my own. Its all about ma Lucy Janey
> Stubbes, And she has caused my heart to mourn, Thar's
> another coon barber from Virginia, In society he's
> the leader of the day, And now ma honey gal is gwine
> to quit me, Yes she's gone and drove this coon away...
> She'd no escuse, To turn me loose, I've been abused, I'm
> all confused, Cause these words she did say...
> All coons look alike to me, I've got another beau,
> you see, And he's just as good to me as you, nig!
> ever tried to be, He spends his money free, I know we
> can't agree, So I don't like you no how, All coons look
> alike to me.

In a real sense Hogan wrote his song in blackface makeup, knowing the expectations of music publishers and the white American public. Hogan also made the eating of watermelon his hallmark routine for minstrel and vaudeville audiences. As the orchestra played the melody of Watermelon Time, Hogan would delight the audience with a pantomime of the best way to devour the succulent fruit.[4]

Giving white audiences the familiar black stage characters allowed Hogan to gradually introduce black music and dance to the public. A year after he wrote his famous (to some his infamous) "coon" song, Hogan organized a minstrel troupe called the Georgia Graduates. The troupe scored a hit with a dance-song performed

by Hogan. Known as the Pas Ma La, the song's lyrics described
how to do the dance.

> Hand upon yo' head, let your mind roll far,
> Back, back, back and look at the stars,
> Stand up rightly, dance it brightly,
> That's the Pas Ma La.

Hogan demonstrated the dance by walking forward and then
hopped back three steps with knees bent. According to dance historian Marshall Stearns, Hogan was the first to incorporate black
folk steps into popular dances of the day.[5]

His success with the Georgia Graduates earned Hogan a featured role with a newly formed troupe managed by white producers. The star of the show, Madame M. Sissierette Jones, was the
best known black soprano in the country. A native of Virginia
whose parents moved to Rhode Island, Jones studied at the New
England Conservatory. She started giving concerts in 1888 (age
19), touring the United States and Europe for eight years. In 1892
she sang at the White House for President Benjamin Harrison, and
later that year she was the star of a concert at Madison Square Garden.

The stage name Black Patti was bestowed on Madame M.
Sissierette Jones in recognition of her rich voice which white con-
noisseurs compared favorably with Adelina Patti, the reigning
caucasian prima donna. In 1896 Jones' white managers (Voelckel
and Nolan) created a vaudeville company called Black Patti's Troubadours. A program from 1898 at the Los Angeles Theatre announced "three hours of Mirth and Melody Beginning with the
Musical Skit, At Jolly 'Coon'-ey Island by Ernest Hogan." Some
clues to Hogan's skit are the names of the 19 characters: Staley
Sausage, a waiter; Miss Aflat Badnote; Cleo De Mudd; Waite Forme;
Percey Nobrains, a masher; and Jim Jollies, the real thing (played
by Ernest Hogan).

The "Coon"-ey Island skit featured ten songs and two dance
numbers. Two songs, My Coal Black Lady and Three Little

Pumpkin Colored Coons, reveal the minstrel show origins of black vaudeville. After five-minute intermission, the Troubadour Sextette sang (no titles on the program). Then "Black Patti (Mme. Sissieretta Jones)" appeared on stage for one aria (Lombardi) by Verdi. Ernest Hogan was next on stage with "his original 'coon' songs, including 'All Coons Look Alike To Me,' 'Pas-Ma-La,' 'Honey You Made a Hit With Me,' Etc., Etc."

After a second five-mintue intermission, the troupe presented "The Operatic Kaleidoscope...Introducing the world-famed Black Patti (Mme. Sissierette Jones) the greatest singer of her race." Aided by a contralto, tenor, baritone, basso and chorus, Black Patti climaxed the evening with selections from Cavalleria Rusticana, Faust, Il Travatore and other familiar opera staples. She changed the pace from heavy arias to national airs: Star Spangled Banner, Dixie, Yankee Doodle, The Campbell's Are Coming.[6]

The odd fusion of minstrel show and grand opera had a more Southern flavor at the Park Theatre in Indianapolis. The Black Patti Troubadours opened the evening with Hogan's At Jolly Cooney Island, followed by James Bland's tune, When He Turns All Black Folks White. Hogan again returned to the footlights with his rendition of If They Only Fought With Razors in the War. "Reminiscences of the Camp and Plantation, by the Troubadours Sextette...dressed as soldiers singing patriotic songs and giving an exhibition drill to the music of war songs."

Black Patti has two solos, My Old Kentucky Home and Suwanee River. Then Hogan has a comic monologue entitled Black Chevalier and a medley of "coon" songs. "Closing feature: Selections from Grand and Comic Opera by Black Patti and Company."[7]

Hogan left the Black Patti troupe a year later to work with Will Marion Cook. Trained as a classical musician in Europe, Cook also studied with Anton Dvorak at the National Conservatory of Music in Washington, D.C. As a young man in his twenties, Cook led a chamber orchestra that toured the eastern United States. His fame as a composer began with the success of his musical-comedy sketch, Clorindy; or, The Origin of the Cakewalk. In his later years,

Cook became the dean of black music, writing nine musical comedies and dozens of songs collected in a 1912 songbook. Written for solo voice and choral groups, Cook's songs "represent an original, distinctive handling of black folk elements," wrote music historian Eileen Southern.

Cook relied on Hogan to recruit the Clorindy cast, stage the dance numbers, and star in the show. Clorindy made Louisiana the site for the origin of the cakewalk, and traced its progress from colored minstrel shows to hugely popular dance contests. Madison Square Garden was the site of the first New York City cakewalk contest in 1897. Featured were "Negro couples in fancy dress" who "pranced and strutted and twirled to rousing music. The winners were chosen on their style, flashiness of movement, elegance of costume, as well as displaying intricate figures and strutting steps."[8]

Most writers trace the cakewalk to holidays on the plantation when slaves performed for the white folks, as well as their own pleasure. Some plantation mistresses gave a prize cake to the best dancers. The slaves understood among themselves that the strutting was a parody of the Grand March in the big house. No doubt a parody of pompous white grandeur at the start, the cakewalk came to symbolize black pride.

Clorindy; or, The Origin of the Cakewalk was the first all-black musical on Broadway, staged at the Casino Roof Garden. Will Marion Cook wrote about the opening night.

> When I entered the orchestra pit, there were only about fifty people on the Roof. When we finished the opening chorus, the house was packed to suffocation. What had happened was that the show downstairs in the Casino Theatre was just letting out. The big audience heard those heavenly Negro voices and took to the elevators. At the finish of the opening chorus, the applause and cheering were so tumultuous that I simply stood there transfixed, unable to move until Hogan rushed down to the footlights and

shouted: "What's the matter, son? Let's go." The Darktown
finale was of complicated rhythm and bold harmonies...My
chorus sang like Russians, dancing meanwhile like Negroes,
and cakewaking like angels, black angels. When the last note
was sounded, the audience stood and cheered for at least ten
minutes.[9]

Hogan's exhibition of the cakewalk in Clorindy entranced the
white social elites. The cream of white New York society, led by
Mr. and Mrs. William K. Vanderbilt, engaged black dancers to
teach the intricacies of cakewalking. For the first time in ballroom
dancing, the black created steps of the cakewalk humbled the European waltz. The white men "imitated a colored man strutting in
a prize contest...head held high, chin up, elbow out, shoulders
thrown back, and, especially prominent, an exaggerated protuber-
ance."

Clorindy also changed the attitude of white producers who
pigeonholed black performers as "colored" versions of the traditional (white) minstrel show. Ernest Hogan brought to the white
audience the flair and excitement of genuine black dance. Hogan
and Cook overturned the Broadway musical modeled on the English light opera chorus which moved, if at all, rather leisurely.
Clorindy gave white producers an insight to the "practice of the
Negro chorus, to dance strenuously and to sing at the same time."
Hogan's influence changed the concept of a singing and dancing
chorus for Broadway musical shows into the next century.

Not everyone greeted the cakewalk with open arms. The Musical Courier ran an editorial: "Society has decreed that ragtime
and cake-walking are the thing, and one reads with amazement
and disgust of historical and aristocratic names joining in this sex
dance, for the cakewalk is nothing but an African danse du ventre,
a milder edition of African orgies."[10]

A year later (1899) Hogan sailed to Australia as the star of M.
B. Curtis' All Star American Minstrels. Pacific tours out of San
Francisco were common for troupes that crossed the country from

New York City. Minstrel companies gained a publicity cachet by performing in Australia. Curtis' troupe opended July 3rd at the Criterion Theatre in Sydney, played for three weeks and sailed to New Zealand.

The local theater critic reviewed the performance for August 31st.

> This afternoon the city streets were enlivened by the parade of the band of the Curtis Afro-American Minstrels and Variety Company, which is to open its Wellington season in the Opera House to-night. Its stars include "the Black Dante (whose art is of the 'right color' and mystifying), the Bronze Patti (a sweet singer), Mr. Ernest Hogan (known as 'the unbleached American').

The troupe returned to Australia, changing its name to Ernest Hogan's Minstrels. The Flashe (newspaper) of Brisbane reported that "Hogan's Negroes at the Theatre Royal are playing to about the biggest house this theatre has known for many years...Ernest Hogan is one of the best comedians we have ever seen."

On the trip back from Australia, Hogan sailed into Honolulu for the finale of the Pacific tour. Hawaii's principal newspaper, Pacific Commercial Advertiser, gave rave notices even before the troupe opened on March 17th (1900) at the Orpheum Theatre. "Ernest Hogan himself needs no introduction. The author of 'All Coons Look Alike to Me' is known around the world...He is the funniest coon, and the most original coon, the coon with the most contagious laugh that ever ate a watermelon or carved a chicken."[11]

Six months after Hogan's enthusiastic reception in Hawaii, he faced a "blood thirsty" white mob during the New York City race riots of 1900. The New York Journal described how Hogan was nearly killed.

> The wild, uncontrolled passion of the mob was best shown on Broadway at 12:30 o'clock this morning, when that popular comedian and song writer, Ernest Hogan was chased

like a wild beast with a pack at his heels. The rioting was wholly unknown to Hogan when he left the Cherry Blossom Grove, where he had been doing his turn as usual. A cry came from Forty-Fourth Street and Eighth Avenue, and a mob of five hundred men, armed with clubs and stones, surged over towards Broadway. Hogan was seen. 'Get the nigger' was the chorus. Hogan dropped his cane and started down Broadway on a run. The mob followed and for the next three minutes it was a life and death race for Hogan.

At Broadway and Thirty-seventh Street Hogan was almost in the hands of his pursuers. It would have been all over with him in a minutes if he had not darted in an open door of the Marlborough Hotel.[12]

Hogan understood that white people assigned African Americans to one of two roles: a happy coon or a dangerous nigger. His survival as a man and a performer depended on compliance with the expectations of the white social order. Hogan, who portrayed the happy coon to perfection, was much in demand. He played a long run at the New York Theatre and toured throughout the country on the Orpheum vaudeville circuit at a salary of $300 per week. In August of 1901 Hogan purchased a three-story house, located at 50 West 134th Street in Harlem.

The Detroit Free Press in March of 1902 praised "Ernest Hogan, the unbleached coon song writer and singer…has made the greatest hit of any artist that has played the New Temple Theatre." A month later the Boston Globe reviewed Hogan in vaudeville at Keith's. "A real coon, one Ernest Hogan, received the lion's share of the attentions of the large audience…His clever way of rendering coon songs created a wild furor."

In October of 1902 the musical comedy Smart Set opened at the Empire Theatre in Newark. Written by Ernest Hogan and Billy McClain, the production had both men as co-stars. McClain had worked with Hogan in the 1899 tour of Australia. Sylvester Russell, the top critic of black theater, praised Smart Set "for the first time in the history of Negro comedy...everything moves with precision, every piece of stage craft is marked with perfection and every deed is a constant flow of wit and humor."

The scenes are all laid in Honolulu, a rich land of beauty and enchantment, with exotic flower girls who sing and dance. Russell noted that Gus Hall, a white man, managed the show. Based on the Newark trial run, Russell predicted "They (Smart Set) can open on Broadway with modesty, unheralded, and run for the rest of the season. It's the real thing. It's the smartest colored comedy ever produced in America."

A week later in Philadelphia, a newspaper review proclaimed "the enormous production of 40 talented performers...had surpassed all Negro comedy companies...It is generally conceded by all who saw the show that it is the greatest Negro show ever seen in this country. The scenery, costumes, pretty girls and up-to-date musical numbers put the Smart Set in the front rank of all colored shows."[13]

The Smart Set company changed cast members over the next years while still retaining its huge popularity. Hogan, working with 24-year-old composer James Reese Europe, created a new show that expanded genuine Southern black music and dance for the white audiences of Broadway. James Reese Europe later emerged as the key figure in the creation of the "Jazz Age." With Hogan's inspiration, Reese wrote the music for a show "that has been called the first public concert of syncopated music in history."

Reese's authentic black music had to be reflected in the name of the new company. Mindful of the international fame of the Fisk Jubilee Singers (who were students from Fisk University in Nashville), Hogan called his troupe the Memphis Students. The group he assembled included no students and no one from Memphis. Scheduled for a two-week run at Hammerstein's Paradise Garden atop the Victoria Theatre on Broadway, the Memphis Students were so sensational that their engagement lasted for five months.

The reviewer for the New York World at the opening night on June 19, 1905, recognized the unique Southern black spirit of the show as compared with the counterfeit blackface minstrels.

> Ernest Hoagn, the Negro singing comedian, assisted by Abbie Mitchell, a comely mulatto with a sweet soprano voice, and twenty-five others who performed a combined function of chorus and orchestra, gave a half hour specialty called, 'Songs of the Black Folk' that came closer than any of tinsel and burnt cork productions that have been seen on Broadway in the last ten years. The roof garden fairly reeked with melody. There was a fervor in the rendering of the songs and chorus that could never have been supplied by white singers.[14]

Hogan's Memphis Students, in the opinion of James Weldon Johnson, were "the first modern jazz band ever heard on a New York stage, and probably on any other stage." The singers and musicians introduced a performance style later adopted by jazz bands and rhythm and blues groups. Each of the instrumentalists (with the exception of winds) sang as they played. The Memphis Students were the first with the concept of the "singing band."

Hogan and Europe had replaced violins which dominated dance orchestras with folk instruments, such as mandolins, guitars and banjos. Another novelty was the use of a saxophone (an instrument used for special effects in European symphonic music). The drummer added to the new sounds by using noisemaking devices in addition to the drums. Also invigorating white Broadway audiences was the performing orchestra that both accompanied the star vocalists and also sang and danced on its own.

The show was topped off by a dancing conductor (an idea adopted by Cab Callaway in Hollywood films). Will Dixon kept his men together by "dancing out the rhythm, generally in graceful. sometimes in grotestque, steps. Often an easy shuffle would take him across the whole front of the band. This style of directing not only got the fullest possible response from the men, but kept them in just the right humor for the sort of music they were playing."[15]

When Smart Set took to the road under the direction of Will Marion Cook, Hogan began rehearsals on a new project in the fall of 1905. Rufus Rastus, Hogan's title for a full-length musical comedy, featured Hogan as the star. He authored the plot and dialogue, as well as wrote much of the music. The story line concerned the misadventures of an actor working his way through a variety of jobs—bootblack, watermelon man and ticket-taker—until he stumbles on a box of oat meal stuffed with money.

The standout song in the show (not written by Hogan), Oh, Say Wouldn't It Be a Dream, had an invisibe chorus that repeated the lyrics as Hogan sang:

> If I could blow a horn and lead a circus band,
> Say wouldn't it be a dream.
> If coons could only rule this United land,
> Say wouldn't it be a dream.
> We'd make Bert Williams President and Walker would be Vice,
> Joe Walcott for the Senate where he'd cut a lot of ice,
> Affairs of State they'd settle with a pair of poker dice,
> Oh, say wouldn't it be a dream.[16]

Theater critic Sylvester Russell, in the March 17, 1906 Indianapolis Freeman, reviewed Rufus Rastus at the American Theatre.

> Congested standing room from the lower floors to the very
> ceiling of the top most gallery…greeted Mr. Ernest Hogan.
> The occasion was Mr. Hogan's appearance in the greatest
> city of them all as an absolute star, with his name displayed
> in shining electric lights and lavishly pictured on paper.

Hogan himself wrote a letter on his hopes for black performers, published in the November 7, 1906 Indianapolis Freeman.

In my troupe there is not a man or woman who cannot read
and write intelligently and grammatically. This is a thing I
require before I employ anyone...The salvation of the Negro race lies in the arts. The Negro is naturally musical...He
is bound to make his mark where given a chance and ultimately will be a credit to America.[17]

While Hogan saw good prospects for black entertainers, a leading lady of Rufus Rastus granted an interview with an unnamed
reporter from the Indianapolis Freeman in which she rejected the
symbol of blackface.

In an interview regarding her (Carita Day) fairness of complexion and the possibilities of bringing her color to a darker
shade, she declared she wouldn't think of using paint to
darken her skin...I tried to explain that Miss Alice Mackey,
the other leading lady, had acquired the art of knowing how
to make up with an even shade of face varnish...Miss Day is
very fair, with chestnut hair that has an African kink...In
Miss Day's particular case this is a problem for the public to
solve when they see Ernest Hogan, made up as black as
possible, making love to Miss Day, who just dotes on looking as white as she can.[18]

When Rufus Rastus closed after a successful tour, Hogan immediately began working on a sequel in 1907. Conceived as a
vehicle for his skills as singer, dancer and comedian, The Oyster
Man opened in New York City on September 25, 1907. Three
months later "Hogan is compelled to leave his Oyster Man Co.
because a general physical breakdown." Hogan was replaced by
another member of the cast for a few months, but The Oyster
Man closed and the company disbanded. The probable cause of
his disabling condition was tuberculosis. Ernest Hogan died in
May of 1909.

Lester Walton who wrote lyrics for some of Hogan's tunes con-
tributed an obituary to the New York Age (newspaper).

> That the stage loses one of its greatest colored
> comedians in the death of Ernest Hogan is admitted by
> all...the colored members of the theatrical profession
> lose one who might be termed in many respects, a 'Moses'
> of the colored theatrical profession...for there is no
> one at this time to take his place.

Walton was right about the comparison of Hogan to Moses. By
transforming the blackface minstrel show into a venue for genuine
black music and dance, Hogan gave white audiences their first
taste of black culture. Fifty years later rhythm and blues (rock and
roll) became the international emblem for American culture.[19]

Walton was mistaken about "no one at this time to take his
place." The vaudeville team of George Walker and Bert Williams
followed in the footsteps of Hogan. They replaced him in the 1898
Broadway production of Clorindy, or, The Origin of the Cakewalk
when Hogan left the show.

George Walker, a native of Lawrence, Kansas, appeared in amateur colored minstrel shows as a child and graduated to circuses
and medicine shows. Recalling his youthful Westward travels with
tent shows, Walker bragged:

> I was quite an entertainer. I could sing and dance, and was
> good at face-making, beating the tambourine, and rattling
> the bones...white people are always interested in what they
> call 'darky' singing and dancing; and the fact that I could
> entertain in that way as no white boy could, made me valu-
> able to the quack doctors as an advertising card."

Traveling with Dr. Waite's medicine show from Kansas, Walker
won a spot in a San Francisco minstrel show and found his future

partner. Nineteen-year-old Bert Williams impressed Walker (one year older) as "a gaunt fellow over six feet, of orange hue, leaning on a banjo, haggling with a manager." Williams, born in Nassau, immigrated to Florida with his parents. The family later settled in Riverside, California.[20]

As a student in high school, Williams used his gift for mimicry to delight classmates and irritate teachers. Once at age 16 he ran away from home, joining a medicine show for a short time as the barker. Williams knew he had a special voice from his years in his church choir. Eventually quitting school, Williams joined an all-black quartet of singing waiters at Riverside's Old Mission Inn.[21]

Williams took a step upward when he auditioned for a small part with Martin and Selig's Minstrels in San Francisco. That was the most fateful event in his career. A short time after he was hired, Williams made friends with George Walker, a new minstrel recruit. The two formed a vaudeville team and began a theatrical adventure over the next 16 years.

At their first engagement in San Francisco's Midway Plaisance, Williams was the straight man to Walker's comic character. When they left California for Chicago, the team reversed roles with Williams in blackface as comic and Walker as a foil. The new combination won an offer from the producers of The Gold Bug, a musical comedy set to open in September (1896) in New York City.

After a five-day run the Gold Bug closed. Williams and Walker next travelled to Boston for roles in a musical farce, A Good Thing. Panned by the critics, the show closed after a week. The pair returned to New York City, joined The Sandow Show, as comic relief for Eugene Sandow, a German-born muscle-builder. For the third time in one month the pair landed on the street when the German flexed his muscles to empty seats.[22]

After a string of short-lived shows, Williams and Walker made a hit in vaudeville at Koster and Bial's Theatre (built in 1870 as Dan Bryant's Opera House). Most vaudeville acts played one week then moved on to another city. From the first night, the comic partners were hailed by the critics. The New York (white) Dramatic Mirror led the reviews:

> Williams and Walker made their first Eastern appearance in high class vaudeville here and scored an immediate success. The dude member of the team (Walker) does various funny walks, and the common everyday nigger (Williams) has only to open his mouth to bring laughs.

Their booking at Koster and Bial's had to be moved to Proctor's Theatre for the holidays in December. In January of 1897, they returned to Koster and Bial's, advertised as "The Two Real Coons." Since most vaudeville shows had a white blackface act, Williams and Walker had to make a unique niche for themselves. White audiences weary of stale blackface routines bought the premise of "real 'coon' business." Williams and Walker did not transcend the traditional minstrel characters—the elegant dude and the common everyday nigger—in their comic roles. They did, however, bring genuine black dance to vaudeville. Enlisting two female dancers, the team topped their act with a rousing grand cakewalk finale.[23]

Williams and Walker's success with the cakewalk in vaudeville led the producers of Clorindy, or The Origin of the Cakewalk, to replace the departing Ernest Hogan with new stars and a new title. Their starring vehicle, Senegambian Carnival (region in West Africa), opened in Boston in August. Within the Carnival was a two-act musical novelty entitled The Origin of the Cakewalk. The librettos for the original and revised show did not survive.

Newspaper reviews do help reconstruct the locale. The first act, decribed by the Cincinnati Inquirer as a "plantation scene"...depicting "primitive slave days with the sunset festivities in the slave quarters. They dance and sing to their hearts' content." The Washington Post focused on Bert Williams performance: "One of the cleverest delineators of Negro characters on the stage, and has no trouble at all keeping his audience in tears of laughter."

"There is a suspicion of a plot, but the audience soon loses sight of it," observed the Boston Globe. The Boston paper also noted "that fund of humor and eccentricity which has made them (Williams and Walker) famous in minstrelsy." As stage characters, Williams and Walker fulfilled the racial expectations of white audiences. Williams played the loyal plantation darky, and Walker recreated the coon dandy: wearing skin-tight trousaloons, a long-tailed coat with padded shoulders and a high ruffled collar.[24]

In their next two productions—A Lucky Coon and The Policy Players—Williams and Walker relied on the formula of the dandy coon tricking the rural coon who won a sizable gambling prize. Mistaken identity provides the plot for the 1901 production of Sons of Ham. The title does not refer to the biblical Ham, but to Hampton J. J. Flam of Swampville, Tennessee. Posing as the long-lost sons of the Tennessee Ham, Williams and Walker schemed to get his money. In a song written by the partners, they poke fun at the "science" of phrenology. The San Francisco Chronicle said: "The best hit of the last night was the 'Phrenologist Coon' which had many encores."

> After feelin' of your bump
> And your face I've read
> By just feelin' in your pocket
> I can tell what's in your head
> Dat's the reason why they call me
> The phrenologist coon.[25]

The 1902 Williams and Walker musical, In Dahomey, had its genesis in San Francisco at the Mid-Winter Fair in 1894. Among the attractions were Turkish dancing girls, performing dogs and natives from Dahomey, Africa. The ship carrying the Africans failed to arrive in time for the opening. Before the delay could hurt the exhibition, the promoters hired a dozen African Americans who posed as Dahomians. Williams and Walker were among the show's "natives." When the genuine Dahomians arrived, the stand-ins were let go.

George Walker recalled his first contact with the real Dahomians:

> It was there, for the first time, that we were brought into close touch with native Africans, and the study of those natives interested us very much. We were not long in deciding that if we ever reach the point of having a show of our own, we would delineate and feature native African characters and still remain American.

In Dahomey, a musical vehicle for the comic and dance talents of Williams and Walker, fused the reality of race on the streets of New York with a stage plot that portrayed America's long discomfort with black people (who had to search for identity in Africa). The plot on the stage concerned a fraudulent scheme by a black syndicate to colonize some land in Dahomey as a haven for dissatisfied American blacks. Such an organization actually transported 6,000 free-born blacks and emancipated slaves to Liberia, beginning in 1821. Founded by white clergy and white politicians opposed to slavery, the American Colonization Society proposed an alternative to both slavery in the South and black equality in the North. Back-to-Africa stirred little enthusiasm among blacks.[26]

When In Dahomey premiered in New York City on February 13, 1903, it was the first all-black show in a Broadway theater. Even before the curtain went up, the color line was challenged as "blacks vied with whites for the best seats in the house, some offering to pay more than the dollar price of the orchestra seats." But the producers' henchmen barred the entrance, directing blacks to the gallery doors around the corner. Enough black patrons balked so that the next day The New York Times reported "there had been times when the trouble-breeders foreboded a race war."

Sylvester Russell wrote an open letter in the Indianapolis Freeman to the management of the New York Theatre:

> The New York Theatre should have expected that some of
> the well-to-do colored families, of the greatest city in America,
> would expect to be accommodated on the lower floor, to see
> Williams & Walker.
> Some of these managers who are drawing the color line are
> Hebrews. No manager with Hebrew blood in his veins should
> draw the color line and expect the Americans to cease dis-
> criminating against Jews in the exclusive hotel and summer
> resorts, when they are drawing the race line themselves.[27]

Williams and Walker played two private detectives from Boston
(Shylock Homestead and Rareback Pinkerton) hired by the president of the Dahomy Colonization Society to locate missing treasure. The pair after arriving in Dahomey disguise themselves in
native costumes. Walker manages to save the black colonizers from
the wrath of the natives who fear the loss of their lands. Walker
gives up his native garb for elegant dandy clothes, wins the office
of governor of Dahomey, and convinces the colonizers to return to
America.

A review in the New York Herald noted that "the piece has
little plot, of course, and in the main is a sort of satire on the
proposition advanced from time to time to colonize the negroes in
Africa." Drawing attention to the story-line, The New York Times
gave high marks to "the book well above the average, for it was, in
its main outlines, an admirably conceived satire on racial foibles."

Two months after its New York debut, the In Dahomey company sailed to England, taking up residence at London's Shaftesbury
Theatre. Lagging ticket sales made the cast nervous about a short
run until Buckingham Palace summoned the players. Performing
at the birthday party for the young Prince of Wales, the company
scored a hit, especially with the cakewalk. London society followed
the lead of the royal family, ensuring full houses for In Dahomey.[28]

The Wiilliams and Walker team returned to an African setting for their next musical production. Set in Abyssinia (the title) where Jasmine Jenkins (Bert Williams) and Rastus Johnson (Walker) escort a group of black Americans on a trip to Addis Ababa, the capitol.

Mistaken identities plague the visit of Rastus Johnson and Jasmine Jenkins to Abyssinia. Ras is mistaken for a rebel chief, and Jas, trying to protect his friend from the officials, grabs a vase from the market stall. The official then charges Jas with theft and explains that the penalty for such a crime is the loss of the offending hand.[29]

After two musical shows that contrasted life for blacks in Africa with America, the vaudeville team emigrated to a small Southern town. Black residents of the town buy land for a pleasure park for the colored people. But a scheming lawyer convinces the group that the land should be sold for a great profit. Located next to a white neighborhood, the park is turned into a site for moonlight musicales and ruckus parties. Finally the whites buy the park known as Bandanna Land.

Bandanna Land played in New York in February of 1908 and toured on the road for a year, with rave reviews from theater critics throughout the country. The touring company had a cast of 75 and 20 musicians. George Walker collapsed on stage in February 1909 and his wife, Aida Overton Walker, took over his role until the show closed two months later. Walker, never regaining his vigor, died three years later. Bert Williams, on his own for the first time in 16 years, organized his last musical comedy, Mr. Lode of Coal. The musical was a financial fiasco for Williams who in the past had relied on his partner to manage their shows.[30]

Without the business sense that Walker brought to the team, Williams gave up the idea of producing black musical comedy. He created a one-man act for vaudeville which caught the attention of Florenz Ziegfeld. The Ziegfeld Follies, started in 1907, had earned praise from critics and overflowing audiences for its female chorus in lavish costumes. Williams, as the sole black man in a show that featured white women, told Ziegfeld about his concerns. In the contract for the 1910 Follies Ziegfeld agreed "that at no time would he (Williams) be on stage with any of the female members of the company." The contact also ruled out Southern towns when Williams went on tour with the Follies.

Bert Williams described his first rehearsal with the Follies cast:

> When Mr. Ziegfeld first proposed to engage me for the
> Follies, there was a tremendous storm in a teacup. Everyone
> threatened to leave; they proposed to get up a boycott if he
> persisted, they said all sorts of things against my personal
> character. But Mr. Ziegfeld stuck to his guns and was quite
> undisturbed by anything that was said.

Black critic Sylvester Russell felt Williams unqiue musical and dance talents were lost "in a vaudeville skit-farce drama written for a lot of white actors with no reputation."

Displeased with integration on stage, a white critic wrote:

> The producer (Ziegfeld) is lacking in taste and
> discretion when he enages a colored man to ap-
> pear in the same company with white men and
> women.[31]

After Williams appeared in the Ziegfeld Follies of 1910, Booker T. Washington (then the most prominent black leader) wrote an article for a magazine. He lauded Williams for hard work in perfecting his stage routine, and rising to the top of show business. In an apparent swipe at W. E. B. DuBois and the newly formed National Association for the Advancement of Colored People, Washington emphasized:

> During all the years I have known Bert Williams, I have
> never heard him whine or cry about his color, or about any

racial discrimination. He has gone right on, in season and
out of season, doing his job, perfecting himself in his work.[32]

Williams spent the next decade as the only black performer in the
Ziegfeld Follies, working along side blackface Eddie Cantor and a
young W.C. Fields. Off stage on the road, Williams had to find
lodgings and restaurants that catered to blacks, even though the
chorus girls had first class hotel rooms. Movie star of the 1930s
W.C. Fields joined the Follies in 1915, and befriended Williams.
Fields portrayed Williams as a lonely man who met with a great
many unpleasantly limiting conditions and, as time went on, he
seemed to feel a craving for a place where he could meet those of
his own profession. He (Williams) would say 'I'm just regulated, I
don't belong.' It was not said in a bitter tone, but it did sound
sadly hopeless.

Isolated as a black performer and dependent on white writers
for skits in the Follies, Williams spent his last years as the sad
blackface clown with grotesque white painted lips. In March of
1922, 46-year-old Bert Williams died. His employer, Florenz
Ziegfeld, quoted in an obituary in the New York World said:

> Whitest Man He Ever Dealt With." In life and in
> death, Williams could not escape the rigors of race
> in America.[33]

Neither Ernest Hogan, George Walker or Bert Williams could transcend the minstrel stage characters demanded by white audiences.
They did, however, initiate the first genuine black music and dance
for white American audiences. At the time Hogan starred in
Clorindy, or The Origin of The Cakewalk, the cakewalk was the
first dance to cross over from black to white society, traveling from
stage musicals to ballrooms. Before the black musicals of Hogan,
Williams and Walker, New Yorkers flocked to operettas imported
from Europe. Ballroom dancing—schottisches, waltzes and cotil-
lions—by the social elite also imitated European fashions.

George Walker introduced the black style to thousands during his years in vaudeville and musicals. A white reviewer described Walker as:

> spick and span Negro, the last world in tailoring, the highest stepper in the smart coon world. How the fellow did prance in the cakewalk, throwing his chest and his buttocks out in opposite directions, until he resembled a pouter pigeon more than a human being.

Although Williams as the sad clown could not strut across the stage, he performed his version of a dance movement popular among blacks in the South. A white dancer, eager to learn from the partners, described Williams "doing a slow loose-jointed mooch dance...a lazy grind...with rotary hip-slinging and maybe a hop or shuffle." Cakewalk contests spread across the country, drawing crowds to ballrooms and turning the comely Fifth Avenue Vanderbilt mansion into a dance mecca for the elite.[34]

When Hogan died in 1909 and Walker in 1911, genuine black dance and music faded from theaters, finding a new venue in dance studios and ballrooms. Beginning with the cakewalk, a dozen new black dances—turkey trot, grizzly bear, chicken scratch, Charleston and the fox trot—from 1910 to the 1920s inaugurated the Jazz Age. White dancers—wriggling, shaking and twisting—borrowed black energy and defined a new American mainstream.

One man, James Reese Europe, worked closely with both Ernest Hogan and Bert Williams. When ballroom dancing became the rage, he created the fox-trot. Ernest Hogan recruited Jim Europe for a two-week engagement of the Memphis Students troupe at Hammerstein's Victoria Theatre in June of 1905. Hogan's novel concept for white audiences was the black tradition of instrumentalists doubling as singers. Hogan hired 25 of the best musicians who performed both as chorus and orchestra. Jim Europe was at the top of Hogan's list. The two-week engagement lasted for over three months.

A white reviewer for the New York World realized the significance of the Memphis Students performance:

> Ernest Hogan, the Negro singing comedian, assisted...by twenty-five others...performed a combined function of chorus and orchestra...the roof garden fairly reeked with melody. There was a fervor in the rendering of the songs and choruses that never could have been supplied by white singers.[35]

Europe later worked with Williams in his last black musical show, writing songs and directing the orchestra. James Reese Europe was 25 when he joined Hogan's troupe in 1905. Born in Mobile, Alabama, Europe moved to Washington, D.C., with his parents at age 9. At that time Washington had the largest black population of any city in the country. For the Europe family, church attendance meant an opportunity to share their musical talents. Mother Lorraine played the piano and knew musical notation. Her husband, Henry, was a self-taught fiddle and banjo player (who composed a hymn for his Baptist church). Jim had music lessons from his parents on a variety of instruments. He then had violin lessons with Joseph Douglass, the grandson of Frederick Douglass (the black abolitionist).

Soon after the close of Bert Williams' final musical, Europe recruited the best musicians in New York City for James Reese Europe's Society Orchestra. Over the next three years, Europe could not keep up with the demand for his orchestra. He formed secondary groups while he played for white society in New York City, Palm Beach, Saratoga and Newport. Most of the better hotels in New York City installed dance floors, and advertised tea dances that lasted from three in the afternoon to six.

An observant journalist described the phenomenon in the October 1913 issue of Current Opinion. Under the title, New

Reflections on the Dancing Mania, he wrote:

> People who have not danced before in twenty years
> have been dancing, during the past summer, af-
> ternoons as well as evenings. Up-to-date restau-
> rants provide a dancing floor so that patrons may
> lose no time while the waiter is changing plates.
> Cabaret artists are disappearing except as inter-
> ludes while people recover their breaths for the
> following number. One wishes either to dance or
> to watch and to criticize those who dance.[36]

A young white couple, Vernon and Irene Castle, performed the
popular American dance steps at the Cafe de Paris in France during the spring of 1913. The audience included Grand Duchess
Anastasia of Russia and rich American vacationers: Goulds,
Vanderbilts and Astors. Among the American tourists at the Cafe
de Paris were leaders in New York fashion and entertainment circles.
Returning to the United States, the Castles had enough contacts
from Paris to organize a busy schedule of private parties in New
York City. The pair demonstrated dance steps currently in vogue—
grizzly bear and turkey trot—and gave individual lessons to the
guests. Irene tutored the males and Vernon the females.

At a private party in 1913 the hostess had hired James Reese
Europe's Society Orchestra to accompany the Castles dance dem-
onstration. After a few dance numbers, the Castles were aston-
ished at Europe's rhythms and the unique sound of the blend of
instruments. They convinced Europe to join the dancing pair "as
their personal musician," and stipulated that any future contract
must include Europe's orchestra.

In the spring of 1914, the Castles asked Jim Europe to join
them on a "Whirlwind Tour" of 30 cities. The Castles and the
musicians had a trial run at the Manhattan Casino in April. One
newspaper account stated that the Castle-Europe performance was
"the finest musical and dance program ever given." Mr. and Mrs.

Vernon Castle were "wizards of dance, who are to terpsichore what Edison is to electricity."

A review in the Musical Leader emphasized Jim Europe's role in the Manhattan Casino program.

> James Reese Europe is a highly talented musician who has studied the folk music of his people...and has accomplished some remarkable things in composition as well as in the training of the orchestra...just as the negro singer has a peculiarly individual tone which vibrates with emotion and which is unique in quality, so the tone of the orchestra has the same thrill, the same vibration.[37]

Shortly before the "Whirlwind Tour," Jim Europe received the music for the Memphis Blues by W. C. Handy. Written for a brass band, the Memphis Blues reflected Handy's early training with colored minstrel bands. After leaving the post of musical director for the famous Mahara's Minstrels, Handy wrote the Memphis Blues, the first of a series of blues songs. Jim Europe experimented on the piano with Handy's piece, sensing in the slower rhythms a new dance step. Acting as dance master as well as music director, Europe worked with the Castles in creating the fox trot. In one nationwide tour during 1914, the Castles made the fox trot the dance sensation of America.

Jim Europe in an interview with a New York Tribune reporter explained how the fox trot grew out of black culture.

> Mr. Castle has generously given me credit for the fox trot...(a) really negro dance, as is the one-step. The one-step is the national dance of the negro, the negro always walking in his dances.

Europe was the first to transfer black blues into the mainstream American culture. Over the next forty years the fox trot was the standard American ballroom dance. It inspired other popular dances and defined the rhythm for many Tin Pan Alley songs.[38]

The cycle of genuine black music and dance for white audiences, began in 1898 with Ernest Hogan in Clorindy, or the Origin of The Cakewalk. George Walker and Bert Williams perfected the cakewalk, converting many thousands of white dancers to the Southern black style. W. C. Handy and Jim Europe introduced the blues and the fox trot to white audiences across the country. In 1923 a black musical, Runnin' Wild, churned the audience by an uproarious free-kicking Charleston. During the decade of the "Roaring Twenties," America embraced the social dancing and music of Southern blacks in the Charleston, the shimmy and the Black Bottom.[39]

When Elvis Presley appeared on the Ed Sullivan Show in 1956, the music and dance of black America (rhythm and blues) had a new white name, rock 'n' roll. Presley's pelvic gyrations were in debt to Earl "Snake Hips" Tucker. Tucker who migrated from the South danced with Duke Ellington and as soloist in Harlem clubs of the 1920s. Presley never heard of Tucker or his dance (Spanking the Baby), but two generations of black dancers established the style adopted by Presley. The cycle from the minstrel show's counterfeit black culture to the quintessential American style was complete.[40]

ENDNOTES

Jim Crow and Tom Thumb

1. George C. D. Odell, Annals of the New York Stage (New York, Columbia University Press, 1927-1949), 15 volumes; "G. C. D. Odell Dies; Expert on Theater," The New York Times, October 18, 1949.

2. Odell, volume 1, 336, volume 3, 354, 400, 446, 468, 472.

3. Sam Dennison, Scandalize My Name: Black Imagery in American Popular Music (New York, Garland Publishing, 1982), 37–39.

4. Odell, volume 3, 631–633.

5. New York Public Library for the Performing Arts.

6. New York Public Library for the Performing Arts.

7. Carl Wittke, Tambo and Bones (Durham, NC, Duke University Press, 1930), 20–32.

8. Eric Lott, Love and Theft: Blackface Minstrelsy and the American Working Class (New York, Oxford University Press, 1993), 18–19.

9. "An Old Actor's Memories," The New York Times, June 5, 1881, 10.

10. Odell, volume 3, 635–675.

11. David Mayer III, Harlequin In His Element: The English Pantomine, 1806—1836 (Cambridge, Harvard University Press, 1969), 94–95.

12. Odell, volume 6, 311.

13. Edward LeRoy Rice, Monarchs of Minstrelsy (New York, Kenny Publishing Company, 1911), 11.

14. Odell, volume 4, 674–675.

15. Edward LeRoy Rice, compilation from biographies of blackface performers.

16. Hans Nathan, Dan Emmett and the Rise of Early Negro Minstrelsy (Norman, University of Oklahoma Press, 1962), 119, 135–142, 215.

17. Nathan, 355–358.

18. Nathan, 107–108, 243–248, 283.

19. A. H. Saxon, P.T. Barnum: The Legend and The Man (New York, Columbia University Press, 1989), 73.

20. Odell, volume 5, 57.

21. Saxon, 74.

22. Saxon, 69–70; Odell, volume 5, 57, 60.

23. Odell, volume 5, 133, 135, 140, 142.

24. Odell, volume 5, 139, 142.

25. Odell, volume 5, 224.

26. Odell, volume 5, 138; Herbert G. Goldman, Banjo Eyes: Eddie Cantor and the Birth of Modern Stardom (New York, Oxford University Press, 1997), 37.

27. Odell, volume 5, 142, 224.

28. Lott, 269.

29. Odell, volume 5, 226.

30. Wittke, 136–137.

31. Odell, volume 5, 307.

32. Odell, volume 5, 377–378.

33. Odell, volume 5, 392.

34. Odell, volume 6, 75.

35. Allardyce Nicoll, Masks, Mimes and Miracles: Studies in The Popular Theatre (New York, Cooper Square Publishers, 1963), 265–277; Allardyce Nicoll, The World of Harlequin (Cambridge, Cambridge University Press, 1963), 9–16, 40–41; H. Diane Russell, Jacques Callot Prints and Related Drawings (Washington, National Gallery of Art, 1975), 105–129.

36. Paul Bouissac, Circus and Culture (Bloomington, Indiana University Press, 1976), 164–166.

37. William Willeford, The Fool and His Scepter (Evanston, Northwestern University Press, 1969), 132–133.

38. Allen R. Myerson, "For the First Time in 151 Years, Baylor Puts a Bounce in Its Step," The New York Times, January 30, 1996

Irishness of It All

1. Edward MacLysaght, The Surnames of Ireland (New York, Barnes & Noble, 1969), 46; George C. D. Odell, Annals of the New York Stage (New York, Columbia University Press, 1931), volume 5, 226.

2. Edward LeRoy Rice, Monarches of Minstrelsy (New York, Kenny Publishing Company, 1911), 39; Odell, volume 5, 393.

3. Carl Wittke, The Irish in America (New York, Russell & Russell, 1970), 7; Kerby A. Miller, Emigrants and Exiles: Ireland and The Irish Exodus to North America (New York Oxford University Press, 1985), 219; Karl S. Bottigheimer, Ireland and The Irish: A Short History (New York, Columbia University Press, 1982), 247; Lawrence J. McCaffrey, The Irish Diaspora in America (Bloomington, Indiana University Press, 1976), 54–55.

4. Andrew M. Greeley, That Most Distressful Nation (Chicago, Quadrangle Books, 1973), 35–36.

5. Historical Statistics of the United States: Colonial Times to 1970 (Washington, Bureau of The Census, 1975), part 1, 106.

6. McCaffrey, 6; John Francis Maguire, The Irish in America (New York, Arno Press and The New York Times, 1969), 438; George W. Potter, To The Golden Door: The Story of the Irish in Ireland and America (Westport, Conn., Greenwood Press, 1973), 168.

7. MacCaffrey, 8.

8. Kerby A. Miller and Paul Wagner, Out of Ireland (Washington, Elliott and Clark Publishing, 1994), 55.

9. Miller and Wagner, 54.

10. Dennis Clark, The Irish in Philadelphia: Ten Generations of Urban Experience (Philadelphia, Temple University Press, 1973), 35.

11. Marjorie R. Fallows, Irish Americans: Identity and Assimilation (Englewood Cliffs, NJ, Prentice-Hall, 1979), 35.

12. Wittke, 129–130.

13. John Cogley, Catholic America (New York, Dial Press, 1973), 54–55, 57.

14. Wittke, 126.

15. Bruce Levine, Half Slave and Half Free: The Roots of The Civil War (New York, Hill and Wang, 1992), 69.

16. Wittke, 152.

17. Robert Ernest, Immigrant Life in New York City, 1825-1863 (Port Washington, NY, Octagon Books, 1949), 153.

18. Cogley, 58–60; "The Mob in New York," The New York Times, July 14, 1863, 1.

19. Jay P. Dolan, The Immigrant Church: New York's Irish and German Catholics, 1815-1865 (Baltimore, Johns Hopkins University Press, 1975), 34–35.

20. Rice's biography of minstrels includes place of birth.

21. Rice, 38, 79; Johm Dizikes, Opera in America: A Cultural History (New Haven, Yale University Press, 1993), 112–115; "Obituary," New York Dramatic Mirror, September 16, 1893, 7; "Minstrels Once Sang Where Old Bank Stood," Brooklyn Daily Eagle, February 13, 1910; Odell, volume 7, 534–535; William D. Griffin, A Portrait of the Irish in America (New York, Scribner, 1981), 10–11, 111; "Last of Hooley's Minstrels Writes," Brooklyn Daily Eagle, February 4, 1934; "Hooley Lies Dead," Chicago Tribune, September 9, 1893; A.T. Andreas, History of Chicago From the Earliest Period to the Present Time (Chicago, The A.T. Andreas Company, 1886) volume 3, 609–610, 665.

22. Rice, 87, 184.

23. Odell, volume 6, 324.

24. Odell, vol. 6, 326–327, 496.

25. Odell,, vol. 6, 588, Vol. 7, 90.

26. Odell, volume 7, 429–430, 632, 680.

27. Bottigheimer, 247.

28. Newspaper clipping at the New York Public Library for the Performing Arts

29. Odell, volume 8, 506–507; Louis D. Scisco, Political Nativism in New York State (New York, Columbia University Press, 1901), 65–67, 90, 100.

30. Dennis Clark, Hibernia America (Westport, Conn., Greenwood Press, 1986), 54; Alfred Connable and Edward Silberfarb, Tigers of Tammany (New York, Holt, Rinehart and Winston, 1967) 153–155, 167; Seymour Mandelbaum, Boss Tweed's New York (Chicago, Ivan R. Dee Publisher, 1990), 92–93; M. R. Werner, Tammany Hall (Garden City NY, Doubleday, Doran and Company, 1928), 134.

31. Odell, volume 9, 76, 609; "Dan Bryant," The New York Times, April 11, 1875, 7.

32. Richard Moody, Ned Harriagn: From Corlear's Hook to Herald Square (Chicago, Nelson-Hall, 1980), 11–12; Charles Hamm, Yesterdays: Popular Songs in America (New York, Norton, 1979), 187.

33. "Edward Harrigan, Old Comedian, Dead," The New York Times, June 7, 1911, 9; Odell, Volume 10, 643; Moody, 47.

34. E. J. Kahn, Jr., The Merry Partners: The Age and Stage of Harrigan and Hart (New York, Random House, 1955), 27–28; Richard Moody, Ned Harriagn: From Corlear's Hook to Herald Square (Chicago, Nelson-Hall, 1980), 87–88; Sam Dennison, Scandalize My Name: Black Imagery in American Popular Music (New York, Garland Publishing, 1982), 283; William T. Leonard, Masquerade in Black (Metuchen NJ, Scarecrow Press, 1986), 256; Charles Hamm, Yesterdays: Popular Songs in America (New York, Norton, 1979), 279.

35. John McCabe, George M. Cohan: The Man Who Owned Broadway (Garden City, Doubleday & Company, 1973), 2–5, 10–13, 42, 51, 57–63, 72–75, 86–87; Ward Moorehouse, George

M. Cohan: Prince of The American Theater (Westport, Conn., Greenwood Press, 1972), 27, 39, 236, 239; "George M. Cohan Dies at Home," The New York Times, November 6, 1942, 20.

36. Lawrence W. Levine. Black Culture and Black Consciousness; AfroAmerican Folk Thought From Slavery to Freeedom (New York, Oxford University Press, 1977), 300–302.

Irving Berlin Titillates

1. Alexander Woollcott, The Story of Irving Berlin (New York, DaCapo Press, 1983), 95.

2. Lawrence Bergreen, As Thousands Cheer: The Life of Irving Berlin (New York, DaCapo Press, 1996), 73; Charles Hamm, Irving Berlin Songs From the Melting Pot: The Formative Years, 1907-1914 (New York, Oxford University Press, 1997), 90–91.

3. Bergreen, 5, 10–13.

4. Bergreen, 15–17, 21–24.

5. Bergreen, 28, 30–31, 35.

6. Kenneth A. Kanter, The Jews on Tin Pan Alley (New York, Ktav Publishing House, 1982), 14–19.

7. Kanter, 30–31, 112–113.

8. Bergreen, 43–46, 52.

9. Bergreen, 52–53.

10. Terry Waldo, This is Ragtime (New York, Hawthorn Books, 1976), 121.

11. Edward A. Berlin, King of Ragtime: Scott Joplin and His Era (New York, Oxford University Press, 1994), 86–115; Bergreen, 121.

12. James H. Dorman, "Shaping the Popular Image of Post-Reconstruction American Blacks: The 'Coon Song' Phenomenon of the Guilded Age," American Quarterly 40 (December 1988), 450–471; Sam Dennison, Scandalize my Name; Black Imagery in American Popular Music (New York, Garland Publishing, 1982).

13. Frank Dumont, The Witmark Amateur Minstrel guide and Burnt Cork Encyclopedia (New York, M. Witmark & Sons,

1905), 1–150; Melvin Patrick Ely, The Adventures of Amos 'n' Andy: A Social History of an American Phenomenon (New York, The Free Press, 1991), 26–63.

14. Frank C. Davidson, The Rise, Development, Decline and Influence of The American Minstrel Show, dissertation, New York University, 1952).

15. Hamm, 71–73, 85.

16. Bergreen, 149–163; Woollcott, 233.

17. Mammy (videorecording) Warner Brothers, 1930.

18. Holiday Inn (videorecording) Paramount, 1942; Bergreen, 393.

19. This is The Army (videorecording) Warner Brothers, 1943; Alex Haley, The Autobiography of Malcolm X (New York, Ballantine Books, 1964), 104–107.

20. Leonard Dinnerstein, Anti-Semitism in America (New York, Oxford University Press, 1994), 132–134.

Gershwin's Racial Profiling

1. George Gershwin Remembered, A&E Cable Television, January 25, 1997.

2. Rhapsody in Blue (videorecording) Warner Brothers, 1945.

3. Edward Jablonski, Gershwin (New York, Doubleday, 1987), 9–10, 12, 14, 16, 21, 28, 35–36.

4. Jablonski, 38–39.

5. David Levering Lewis, When Harlem Was in Vogue (New York, Alfred A. Knopf, 1981), 98–103.

6. Carl Van Vechten, Nigger Heaven (New York, Harper & Row, 1971), 89–90, 285–287.

7. Joan Peyser, The Memory of All That: The Life of George Gershwin (New York, Simon and Schuster, 1993), 72.

8. Jablonski, 62–63.

9. Jablonski, 75.

10. George Gershwin Remembered; Peyser, 221–222.

11. Jablonski, 6.

12. Jablonski, 203–205.

13. Jablonski, 91.

14. Peyser, 132; "Nazis' Hunt Arms In Einstein Home," The New York Times, March 21, 1933, 10.

15. "Music Hurt by Nazis, Two Composers Say," The New York Times, June 12, 1933, 20.

16. Donald Warren, Radio Priest: Charles Coughlin, the Father of Hate Radio (New York, The Free Press, 1996), 132–135.

17. Jablonski, 194–195.

18. Hollis Alpert, The Life and Times of Porgy and Bess (New York, Alfred A. Knopf, 1990), 74–75.

19. Alpert, 20; Peyser, 223–224.

20. Jablonski, 254.

21. DuBose Heyward, Porgy (New York, Doubleday & Company, 1925).

22. George Gershwin and DuBouse Heyward, Porgy and Bess (New York, Gershwin Publishing Company, 1958).

23. Heyward, 113, 115.

24. Gary D. Engle, This Grotesque Essence: Plays from the American Minstrel Stage (Baton Rouge, Louisiana State University Press, 1978), 1, 9–11.

25. "George Gershwin, Rhapsody in Catfish Row," The New York Times, October 20, 1935, Sec. 10, 1.

26. Eileen Southern, The Music of Black Americans (New York, W.W. Norton, 1997), 460–461; The Story of Gospel, PBS Television, February 2, 1998.

27. Alpert, 160–161, 173, 184, 208, 211.

28. Porgy and Bess: An American Voice, PBS Television, February 4, 1998.

29. Alpert, 121–122.

Jews in Blackface

1. Robert C. Toll, Blacking Up: The Minstrel Show in Nineteenth Century America (New York, Oxford University Press,

1974), 33.

2. Neal Gabler, An Empire of Their Own: How The Jews Invented Hollywood (New York, Crown Publishers, 1988), 3; David R. Roediger, The Wages of Whiteness: Race and the Making of the American Working Class (London, Verso, 1991), 117.

3. Herbert G. Goldman, Jolson: The Legend Comes to Life (New York, Oxford University Press, 1988), 146.

4. Gabler, 1–3.

5. Goldman (Jolson), 301–302.

6. Goldman (Jolson), 9–25.

7. The Jolson Story (videorecording) Columbia Pictures, 1946.

8. Goldman (Jolson), 14, 28; Irving Zeidman, The American Burlesque Show (New York, Hawthorn Books, 1967), 48.

9. New York Dramatic Mirror, December 21, 1889.

10. Goldman (Jolson), 325–328.

11. Letter from The Boston Historical Society.

12. Brooklyn Daily Eagle, February 7, 1909, 8.

13. The New York Times, August 15, 1908, 1.

14. William E. Walling, "The Race War in The North," The Independent 65, September 3, 1908, 529–534.

15. Roberta Senechal, The Sociogenesis of a Race Roit: Springfield, Illinois, in 1908 (Urbana, University of Illinois Press, 1990), 97, 101, 106, 170–173.

16. The New York Dramatic Mirror, November 21, 1908.

17. Goldman (Jolson), 54–60.

18. Brooks McNamara, The Shuberts of Broadway (New York, Oxford University Press, 1990), 5, 8, 35, 61–63.

19. Leonard Dinnerstein, Anti-Semitism in America (New York, Oxford University Press, 1994), 85–87.

20. Gabler, 136–137.

21. Kevin Brownlow, Behind the Mask of Innocence (New York, Alfred A. Knopf, 1990), 374.

22. Brownlow, 378–379, 409–414; Priscilla Fishman, The Jews of The United States (New York, Quadrangle/The New York Times Book Company, 1973), 58.

23. The Jazz Singer (videorecording) Warner Brothers, 1927.

Jolson the Shlemiel

1. The Singing Fool (videorecording) Warner Brothers, 1928.
2. Gabler, 19–21.
3. Mammy (videorecording) Warner Brothers, 1930.
4. Carl Wittke, Tambo and Bones (Durham, NC, Duke University Press, 1930), 103–104.
5. Big Boy (videorecording) Warner Brothers, 1930.
6. Wonder Bar (videorecording) Warner Brothers, 1934. 7. "The Green Pastures," Masterplots II (Pasadena, Salem Press, 1990), 717–721
8. Go Into Your Dance (videorecording) Warner Brothers, 1935.
9. The Singing Kid (videorecording) Warner Brothers, 1936.
10. Goldman (Jolson), 372–373.
11. The Jolson Story (videorecording) Columbia Pictures, 1946.
12. David T. Brigham, "Two Death Camps Places of Horror," The New York Times, July 6, 1944.
13. Goldman (Jolson), 301–302.
14. Goldman (Jolson), 145–149.
15. Herbert G. Goldman, Banjo Eyes: Eddie Cantor and the Birth of Modern Stardom (New York, Oxford University Press, 1997), 37–40.
16. Gabler, 35–38.
17. Whoopee (videorecording) Samuel Goldwyn, 1930.
18. Roman Scandals (videorecording) Samuel Goldwyn, 1933.
19. Kid Millions (videorecording), Samuel Goldwyn, 1934.
20. Babes in Arms (videorecording) MGM/UA Home Video, 1966.
21. Babes on Broadway (videorecording) MGM/UA Home Video, 1968.

22. Sally F. Moore and Barbara G. Myerhoff, Secular Ritual (Amsterdam, Van Gorcum, Assen, 1977), 3–12, 199–200.

Strutting to Redemption

1. Odell, vol. 8, 353; vol. 9, 501.

2. Mel Watkins, On The Real Side: Laughing, Lying and Signifying (New York, Simon & Schuster, 1994), 125; Eileen Southern, The Music of Black Americans (New York, Norton & Company, 1997), 229.

3. Southern, 302; Shane White and Graham White, Stylin' African American Expressive Culture from Its Beginnings to the Zoot Suit (Ithaca, Cornell University Press, 1999), 66, 72, 154.

4. Henry T. Sampson, The Ghost Walks: A Chronological History of Blacks in Show Business, 1865-1910 (Metuchen NJ, The Scarecrow Press, 1988), 110; Nathan Huggins, Harlem Renaissance (New York, Oxford University Press, 1971), 277.

5. Lynne F. Emery, Black Dance from 1619 to Today (Princeton, Princeton Book Company, 1988), 205; Marshall and Jean Stearns, Jazz Dance (New York, Da Capo Press, 1994), 101–102, 119. 6. Sampson (Ghost), 146–147; Southern, 246, 301-302.

7. Sampson (Ghost), 165.

8. Southern. 272–274; Huggins, 273; Stearns, 122.

9. David Krasner, Resistance, Parody and Double Consciousness in African American Theatre (New York, St. Martin's Press, 1997), 78–79; Southern, 302.

10. Thomas L. Riis, Just Before Jazz: Black Musical Theater in New York, 1890-1915 (Washington, Smithsonian Institution, 1989), 80; Emery, 208; Stearns, 122–123.

11. Sampson (Ghost), 179, 183, 200, 203–204, 206, 210.

12. Sampson (Ghost), 221–222.

13. Sampson (Ghost), 235, 250–251, 275.

14. Reid Badger, A Life in Ragtime: A Biography of James Reese Europe (New York, Oxford University Press, 1995), 29–30; Southern, 302; Sampson (Ghost), 345.

15. Riis, 39; Southern, 345–346.

16. Riis, 125–127.

17. Sampson (Ghost), 362, 378.

18. Sampson (Ghost), 390.

19. Sampson (Ghost), 422, 465; Riis, 39.

20. Huggins, 280; Eric L. Smith, Bert Williams, A Biography of the Pioneer Black Comedian (Jefferson, NC, McFarland & Company, 1992), 229–230.

21. Smith, 4–7.

22. Smith, 9–10, 13; Riis, 44.

23. Smith, 26.

24. Smith, 34–35.

25. Smith, 40–41, 43–45, 47.

26. Smith. 14–15; Krasner, 66. 27. Smith, 55; Sampson (Ghost), 288, 292.

28. Huggins, 281; Riis, 51, 91–92, 103.

29. Smith, 86.

30. Mable Rowland (editor), Bert Williams: Son of Laughter—(New York, Negro Universities Press, 1969), 65; Riis, 117; Sampson (Ghost) 451, Smith, 94.

31. Smith, 132–133,

32. Smith, 145–146.

33. Smith, 175, 291.

34. Emery, 211–212; Gerald Jonas, Dancing; The Pleasure, Power and Art of Movement (New York Harry N. Abrams, Inc., 1992), 174; Stearns, 124.

35. Badger, 30.

36. Badger, 10, 16–17, 19, 42, 82–83.

37. Badger, 80, 82, 103, 107.

38. Badger, 115–116; Southern, 338; Stearns, 98.

39. Southern, 440; Stearns, 145.

40. Emery, 233–234; Rock 'n' Roll (videorecording) WGBH Educational Foundation and the BBC, 1995; The History of Rock 'n' Roll (videorecording) volumes 1 and 2, Time-Life Video, 1995.